Madeira Walks

(Volume One of a Walk! Series)

Leisure Trails

with

Shirley & Mike Whitehead

DISCOVERY WALKING GUIDES LTD

Madeira Walks: Volume One, Leisure Trails

First edition published May 2015
Reprinted August 2016
Second Edition published April 2019

Published by
Discovery Walking Guides Ltd
10 Tennyson Close, Northampton NN5 7HJ, England

Maps
Maps sections are taken from **Madeira Tour & Trail Map** published by **Discovery Walking Guides Ltd**.

Photographs
The photographs in this book were taken by the authors and co-walkers.

Front Cover Photographs

Walk 25: Levada do Risco
Walk 1: descending to Câmara de Lobos
Walk 26: Levada do Alecrim
Walk 19: The central mountain range from the Balcões

Text and photographs © Shirley & Mike Whitehead
Maps © David Brawn

ISBN 9781782750581

All rights reserved. No part of this publication may be reproduced, stored in a retrieval system or transmitted in any form or by any means, electronic, mechanical, photocopying, recording or otherwise, without the prior written permission of the publishers.

The author and publishers have tried to ensure that the information and maps in this publication are as accurate as possible. However, we accept no responsibility for any loss, injury or inconvenience sustained by anyone using this book.

Madeira Walks
(volume one)
CONTENTS

Contents	3
The Authors	7
Acknowledgements	7
Preface	8
Introduction	9
Topography	9
Climate	9
The Levadas	9
Flora and Fauna	**10**
Walking	**11**
Getting Around	**13**
Places to Visit & Other Things To Do	**13**
Symbols Rating Guide	**19**
Map Information	
Walk Locator Maps	**20 & 21**
Map Notes & Legend	**22**
Using GPS on Madeira	**23**

THE WALKS

WALKS IN FUNCHAL & THE CENTRAL REGION

1 Praia Formosa to Câmara de Lobos — 24
  1 walker, 1¼ hours, 3km, ascents/descents negligible, vertigo risk 0, refreshments 4 (linear one way, circular with bus)

2 Romeiros to Jasmin Tea House and Palheiro Gardens — 28
  1 walker, 2 hours, 8km, ascents negligible, descents 100 metres, vertigo risk 1, refreshments 2 (linear one way, circular with bus)

3 Levada do Norte & Levada da Rabaças - Encumeada — 31
  1 walker, 2 hours, 6km, ascents & descents negligible, vertigo risk 1, refreshments 1 (linear out and back)

4 Levada do Norte: Estreito de Camera de Lobos - Cabo Girão — 34
  2 walker, 2½ hours, 8km, ascents 45 metres, descents negligible, vertigo risk 1, refreshments 2 (linear one way)

5 Levada dos Piornais - Madeira Shopping to Funchal Lido area — 37
  3 walker, 3½ hours, 9km, ascents negligible, descents 240 metres, vertigo risk 3, refreshments 4 (linear one way)

6 Levada dos Piornais - Santa Rita circular — 40
  2 walker, 2 hours, 5km, ascents & descents 160 metres, vertigo risk 3, refreshments 1 (circular)

7	**Eira do Serrado to Curral das Freiras (Nun's Valley)**	41

2 walker, 1¼ hours, 2.5km, ascents negligible, descents 405 metres, vertigo risk 0, refreshments 2 (linear one way)

8	**Ecological Park to Monte (PR 3.1 Caminho Real do Monte)**	44

3 walker, 2 hours, 5km, ascents 30 metres, descents 620 metres, vertigo risk 0, refreshments 3 (linear one way, circular with bus)

9	**Monte - Bom Sucesso - Funchal**	48

3 walker, 2 hours, 7km, ascents 20 metres, descents 550 metres, vertigo risk 2, refreshments 0 (circular, with bus/Teleférico)

10	**Levada dos Tornos Monte - Babosas - Curral Romeiros**	51

3 walker, 1 hour 50 mins, 6km, ascents & descents 200 metres, vertigo risk 3, refreshments 3 (circular)

WALKS IN SOUTH EAST AND NORTH EAST REGION

11	**Levada da Azenha - Caminho Velho do Castelo (PR23)**	54

1 walker, 1 hour, 2.6km, ascents & descents negligible, vertigo risk 0, refreshments 1 (linear out and back)

12	**São Lourenço: Prainha - Pico da Piedade**	56

1 walker, 1 hour, 3km, ascents & descents 120 metres, vertigo risk 0, refreshments 1 (circular)

13	**Arco de São Jorge to Boaventura**	59

2 walker, 1¾ hours, 4km, ascents 230 metres, descents 200 metres, vertigo risk 0, refreshments 2 (linear one way)

14	**Santana - Fajá da Rocha do Navio**	62

2 walker, 2 hours, 6km, ascents 50 metres, descents 420 metres, vertigo risk 1, refreshments 1 (circular, with Teleférico)

15	**Levada do Caniçal (East)**	65

2 walker, 1½ hours, 5km, ascents 20 metres, descents 230 metres, vertigo risk 0, refreshments 2 (linear one way)

16	**Levada do Castelejo, São Roque**	68

2 walker, 3 hours, 8km, ascents & descents 50 metres, vertigo risk 0, refreshments 0 (linear out and back)

17	**Pico do Facho - Machico**	71

3 walker, 1¼ hours, 3km, ascents 90 metres, descents 320 metres, vertigo risk 0, refreshments 2 (linear one way)

18	**The Old Trail to Caniçal**	73

2/3 walker, 2 hours, 5.5km, ascents 90 metres, descents 310, metres, vertigo risk 0, refreshments 2 (linear one way)

WALKS IN CENTRAL EAST REGION

19	**Vereda dos Balcões - (PR11)**	76

1 walker, ¾ hour, 3km, ascents & descents negligible, vertigo risk 0, refreshments 3 (linear out and back)

20   Santana - Pico das Pedras to Queimadas   78
1 walker, 1¼ hours, 5km, ascents & descents negligible, vertigo risk 0, refreshments 1 (linear out and back)

21   Abrigo de Pastor Circular - Poiso   81
1 walker, 1½ hours, 4km, ascents & descents 120 metres, vertigo risk 0, refreshments 1 (circular)

22   Santo da Serra - Serrado das Ameixieras - Madre de Agua   84
2 walker, 2½ hours, 8km, ascents & descents 100 metres, vertigo risk 0, refreshments 1 (circular)

23   Pico do Areeiro - Juncal Viewpoint - Ninha da Manta   87
2 walker, 1½ hours, 3km, ascents & descents 150 metres, vertigo risk 0, refreshments 1 (linear out and back)

24   Levada do Furado (PR10) Ribeiro Frio to Portela   90
3 walker, 3½ hours, 11km, ascents negligible, descents 200 metres, vertigo risk 1, refreshments 2 (linear one way)

24A   Levada do Furado: Ribeiro Frio to Santa da Serra   93
3 walker, 4 hours, 14km, ascents neg. descents 190 metres, vertigo risk 1, refreshments 2 (linear one way)

WALKS IN CENTRAL WEST REGION

25   Rabaçal: Levada do Risco (PR6.1)   95
1 walker, 2 hours, 4.2km, ascents 20 metres, desents 240 metres, vertigo risk 0, refreshments 0 (linear out and back)

26   Rabaçal: Ribeira Grande   97
1 walker, 2 hours, 6km, ascents & descents 20 metres, vertigo risk 1, refreshments 0 (linear out and back)

27   Levada do Paul - Cristo Rei - Fátima Chapel, Rabaçal   100
1 walker, 3½ hours, 10km, ascents & descents negligible, vertigo risk 0, refreshments 1 (linear out and back)

28   Around Fanal   103
1 walker, 1¼ hours, 4km, ascents & descents 70 metres, vertigo risk 0, refreshments 0 (circular)

29   Cristo Rei - Levada Bica da Cana   105
2 walker, 2 hours, 6km, ascents & descents negligible, vertigo risk 1, refreshments 0 (linear out and back)

30   Vereda das Chão dos Louros - São Vicente Valley (PR22)   108
1 walker, 1¼ hours, 1.9km, ascents & descents 60 metres, vertigo risk 0, 0 refreshments (circular)

31   Estanquinhos to Pico Ruivo do Paúl   111
3 walker, 2 hours, 5km, ascents & descents 170 metres, vertigo risk 0, refreshments 0 (figure of eight circular)

| 32 | **Fanal to Curral Falso - (PR14 Levada dos Cedros)** | 114 |

2 walker, 5 hours, 11.6km, ascents & descents 290 metres, vertigo risk 1, refreshments 0 (linear out and back)

| 33 | **Curral Falso to Ribeira da Janela - (PR15)** | 117 |

2 walker, 1½ hours, 2.7km, ascents negligible, descents 440 metres, vertigo risk 0, refreshments 1 (linear one way)

| 34 | **Bica da Cana - Pináculo - Bica da Cana** | 120 |

3 walker, 2½ hours, 6km, ascents & descents 160 metres, vertigo risk 1, refreshments 0 (circular)

| 35 | **Levada das 25 Fontes (PR6) via Calheta Tunnel** | 123 |

3 walker, 3 hours, 8km, ascents & descents 70 metres, vertigo risk 2, refreshments 0 (linear out and back)

WALKS IN SOUTH WEST AND NORTH WEST REGION

| 36 | **Levada do Moinho - Achadas da Cruz - circular** | 126 |

1 walker, 2 hours, 6km, ascents & descents 100 metres, vertigo risk 1, refreshments 2 (circular)

| 37 | **Santa - Porto Moniz** | 129 |

2 walker, 1½ hours, 5km, ascents negligible, descents 462 metres, vertigo risk 0, refreshments 5 (linear one way)

| 38 | **Levada Nova - Fajã da Ovelha to Ponta do Pargo** | 132 |

2/3 walker, 3 hours 10 mins, 10km, ascents 0m, descents 150 metres, vertigo risk 0, refreshments 1 (linear one way)

| 39 | **Levada da Ribeira da Janela -Lamaceiros** | 136 |

3 walker, 4 hours, 12km, ascents & descents negligible, vertigo risk 1, refreshments 1 (linear out and back)

| 40 | **Ponta do Pargo to Cabo** | 139 |

2 walker, 3¼ hours, 8km, ascents & descents 225 metres, vertigo risk 0, refreshments 1 (linear out and back)

| 41 | **Fajã da Ovelha -Paúl do Mar** | 142 |

3 walker, 2¼ hours, 7km, ascents 20 metres, descents 610 metres, vertigo risk 0, refreshments 2 (linear one way)

| | **Glossary** | 145 |

Appendices

A	Useful Information	146
B	Gardens,Nature Reserves, Natural History Museums, Festivals & Events	147
C(1)	Official Recommended Trails For Hikers	149
C(2)	Disabled Routes	149
D	Reference Sources	150
E	Bus Information	151

Place Names Index   153

THE AUTHORS

Shirley and Mike Whitehead settled in Madeira in 2002 and live in Jardim do Mar on the south west coast. Both born in Lancashire England, they lived for many years in Yorkshire where they pursued their interest in walking and the environment, particularly in West Yorkshire and the Yorkshire Dales.

Since moving to Madeira they have spent much of their time discovering the island's diverse landscape and its natural and cultural history, walking the levadas, forest trails, moorland and mountain tracks and coastal routes as well as visiting many of the towns, villages and hamlets across the island.

Their previous walking guides **Shirley Whitehead's Madeira Walks** and **Walk! Madeira** with Shirley & Mike Whitehead were published by Discovery Walking Guides Ltd with subsequent editions produced in 2011 and 2012 respectively.

Acknowledgements

Our sincere thanks to our co-walker Alan Wood for his help, support and enthusiasm.

PREFACE

As a walker's paradise, Madeira has it all - majestic mountains, rugged coastline, ancient forests, a unique *levada* network and verdant flora; easy to see why so many walkers return year after year. Over the past decade, the island's infrastructure and facilities have undergone extensive development; not least has been the substantial investment to improve walking trails helping make Madeira one of Europe's top hiking destinations.

To date, the regional government has designated thirty routes on Madeira as 'Recommended Trails for Hikers' and currently **Walk! Madeira** and **Shirley Whitehead's Madeira Walks** are the only publications to recognize this development by the inclusion of these trails in our guides. Leading on from this, we now believe it's time to re-organise our books again, this time into a compendium of two new editions graded as follows. **Walk! Madeira - Volume 1** includes leisure routes and easier walking trails whilst **Walk! Madeira - Volume 2** covers the more challenging and high altitude routes. Both books are arranged by geographic area then listed by exertion rating under each area.

In both editions we have taken into account the relevant official trails and have introduced a number of new routes as well as including our favourite 'off the beaten track' walks; regardless of fitness, age or ability, there's something for everyone.

All routes included have been surveyed and mapped using GPS satellite navigation. The authors and their co-walkers have walked all the trails, ensuring accuracy and up to date information. Clear descriptions guide the walker both to the starting point of the walks and throughout the routes, with gradings, distances, timings and altitudes all symbolized. Information on flora and fauna is also included, while references to places of interest give readers a sense of the culture and history around these trails. Map sections were developed from the **Madeira Tour & Trail Map**, by far the most up to date and best-selling map on the island.

INTRODUCTION

Madeira is a wonderful destination for walkers offering a truly breathtaking diversity of landscape; its lushly vegetated slopes, towering volcanic peaks, dramatic gorges and soaring cliffs, all take visitors by surprise. Add to this the *levada* network, the primeval forests, the subtropical flora and the superb landscaped gardens - little wonder then that the island is often referred to as "The floating garden of the Atlantic".

The north coast

TOPOGRAPHY

The archipelago is situated in the eastern Atlantic, around 950 kilometres south of mainland Portugal and 600 kilometres west of Morocco. It consists of the principal island of **Madeira, Porto Santo**, the **Desertas** and the **Salvagens;** the latter two being uninhabited nature reserves protected by the **Parque Natural da Madeira**. Together with the Azores, Canaries and the Cape Verde Islands, these archipelagos form a bio-geographic region referred to as Macaronesia.

With a population of 267,000 Madeira's economy consists of small to medium size industry, tourism and some agriculture, mostly wine. The main island is around 57 kilometres long and 23 kilometres wide; the central massif includes the peaks of **Pico Ruivo (1862m), Pico Areeiro (1818m)** and **Pico das Torres (1852m).** The north coast boasts tall sea cliffs; the most extreme is **Cabo Girão** on the south coast, being the highest in Europe and second highest in the world. The neighbouring island of **Porto Santo** is renowned for its magnificent sandy beach, nine kilometres long.

CLIMATE

Madeira enjoys a temperate year round climate with average daytime temperatures around the coast of 18°C-24°C. Generally speaking, the north is wetter and cloudier than the south, while along the island's mountainous spine, the weather is subject to rapid change and can be windy, wet and cloudy - and occasionally, snowy. There's a useful website (www.netmadeira.com) giving hourly updates, via web cam photographs, on weather conditions across the island.

THE LEVADAS

Although irrigation channels are not unique to Madeira, the island undoubtedly boasts some of the world's finest examples. There are over 200 *levadas,* covering 1500 kilometres, with new channels still being constructed. Historically built for irrigation to bring water from the wetter north to the arid southern areas, the *levadas* later became important for hydropower. Most slope gently - almost imperceptibly in some cases - as they follow the natural contours of the terrain, providing ideal walking where accompanying paths allow. Where the shape of the land gets in the way, tunnels have been pushed through to take the channels. From the walker's point of view, the *levadas* not only provide memorable and beautiful walking experiences, they open up

A carved tunnel carries a *levada*

otherwise impenetrable regions of the island's interior.

Levadeiros (Levada Workers) are charged with keeping the channels and pathways in good condition and the levada keeper's cottages, usually surrounded by well-planted gardens, can be found along many of the routes.

FLORA AND FAUNA

Protea species from South Africa

The Laurisilva
The island's name means 'wood', so named by early settlers who found it almost totally covered by great forests of mainly Lauraceae species, but over the centuries the trees were used for timber and the lower woodlands were burnt to release land for farming and pastures.

Echium Candicans, Paúl da Serra

Newer forests of pine, acacia (Mimosaceae), eucalyptus and oak now occupy much of the *laurisilva*'s former territory. Nevertheless, the natural forest of Madeira is the largest area of *laurisilva* in the world. It covers 150 sq. km (58 square miles) representing just over 20% of the island's surface. Many of the plants evolved millions of years ago and the **laurisilva** survives now only in Central Macaronesia.

Due to their importance these subtropical humid forests were classified a World Nature Heritage Site in 1999 by UNESCO.

Plants and Trees
Given its climate and the fertility of the volcanic soil, Madeira is a botanical paradise renowned for its luxurious sub-tropical vegetation, where species from around the world thrive in the gardens and avenues. There are over 1300 species of indigenous and naturalized plants of which around 150 are endemic. Vineyards and banana plantations dominate the lower coastal areas and along the agricultural terraces you'll find exotic fruit trees of papaya, fig, mango, avocado, orange and lemon. The main vegetable crops include sweet potato, beans, tomatoes and various types of brassicas.

Birds
There are a number of Important Bird Areas (IBAs) within the archipelago with around 250 bird species and subspecies recorded, some 42 of which breed regularly. The only true endemics are the long-toed pigeon (Columba trocaz), which inhabits the *laurisilva,* and the Zino's petrel (Pterodroma Madeira), breeding on the cliff tops and mountains. There are however a number of endemic sub-species, as well as Macaronesian endemics. SPEA-Madeira is the Portuguese Society for the Protection of Birds and is a partner of Birdlife International. Information on publications for bird watching areas is given in Appendix D.

Monarch butterfly

Animals
No mammals other than bats occur naturally. The only endemic reptile species is the Madeiran Wall Lizard (Teira dugesii).

Insects include grasshoppers, crickets and migratory locusts, plus many butterflies, the beautiful Monarch being the largest species on the island.

Aquatic mammals include a number of species of whales and dolphins, which can sometimes be observed from the coastal areas, and the endangered Mediterranean Monk Seal, now thriving around the **Desertas** islands and occasionally seen off the coastline of Madeira; turtles are also quite commonly seen in the coastal waters.

WALKING
Madeira is a beautiful and safe destination for walkers, but being an isolated island in the Atlantic, problems with extreme weather do occur from time to time resulting in the temporary closure of walking trails. The tourist offices and hotels are kept up to date with the status of routes; you can also go online at **www.visitmadeira.pt** - click useful information on the home page, then click footpaths and *levadas* then trekking, to access the current status of the official walking trails.

Obviously from time to time, walking routes do change, some are minor whilst others more important, particularly where safety is concerned. For this purpose we recommend you visit www.discoverywalking.com, scrolling down to Madeira Walking - Latest Updates, or simply follow this link:

https://bit.ly/2Txkt3c

Trails and Paths
The selection of routes included in this publication provide an easy introduction to walking in Madeira and are classed as pleasant leisure walks to easier, yet still challenging trails. We have also taken into account comments received from walkers over the last few years by including more circular routes, more walks in and around Funchal and trails easily accessible by bus.

We believe that these routes provide something for everyone, regardless of individual ability and fitness. There's a good balance including coastal routes, forest trails, moorland and mountain pathways and *levada* walks. The terrain on routes varies widely. Some *levada* walks, although long, are on flat, easy paths with negligible ascents and descents; others require more concentration where there are narrow paths, with mildly precipitous sections.

Madeira Walks - Volume 1 includes the whole or sections of 14 of the official walking trails, (See the following paragraph for details). The remainder of the official routes are included in **Madeira Walks - Volume 2**.

The official "Recommended Trails for Hikers".
Over the past decade, the island's infrastructure and facilities have undergone extensive development; not least has been the substantial investment to improve walking trails helping make Madeira one of Europe's top hiking destinations.

Twenty nine routes on Madeira plus two on Porto Santo have been designated 'Recommended Trails for Hikers' by the Regional Government, all being upgraded, signed and made safer for the public.

One of the PR route information panels

This programme of 'Access for All' continues to increase the scope and variety of walking routes throughout the island, with a number now created specifically for disabled people, using the unique 'Joelette' cycles. One route for blind people and three additional routes for cyclists have also been created. See Appendix C for details.

Preparation
Be prepared - read through the walk description before you set out, and take note of the information bar for each route. Also make sure you have planned your return journey from the end of the walk, particularly if traveling by bus.

The time taken for each route is obviously relative to age, personal fitness and preference. Our times are the recorded walking times and do not include stops for taking photos, resting or refreshments so we recommend that you add around 25% to timings to cover stoppages.

Distance is shown in kilometres, and ascents and descents in metres. Routes are shown as one-way, out and back or circular. Vertigo risk ranges from 0 (no risk) to 3 (high vertigo risk). Note that the vertigo risk often applies to only a short section of the route, although if you're a sufferer, this could feel like the longest few metres you've ever walked. (See symbols ratings guide).

Safety - Do take safety seriously:-

Please note that there is no organised mountain rescue service in Madeira; incidents are dealt with by a combination of Ambulance, Fire and Police services. The Regional Government accepts no responsibility for personal injury or damage of property and therefore we are individually responsible for our own safety. We suggest the following checklist:-

- Don't take risks. If you find a route made impassable by, for example, a landslide, then turn back. Attempting to find your own way through can be highly dangerous, especially on newly fallen slides. Look for the signs; if the landslip has been levelled or boarded by the *Levadeiros*, then it is usually safe to cross.

- Take note of local weather forecasts (remember that weather changes happen swiftly on mountainous islands, especially at altitude). Turn back if bad weather sets in.

- Start out early and plan to finish well before dusk. Let someone know (at your hotel, for example) where you plan to walk and what time you expect to be back, and if possible walk with a companion.

- Go properly equipped with an up to date map and guidebook and a torch for all routes with tunnels. GPS is desirable but not essential: a compass at least is recommended on moorland and high altitude routes.

- Clothing, including footwear, should be up to the job and should include a light raincoat and fleece when going into the mountains.

- Take lots of water with you and food on longer walks

- If possible take a mobile phone and emergency contact numbers although you should bear in mind that mobile phones may not always work in remote parts of the island.

GETTING AROUND

Hire cars and taxis are the most convenient way of getting around and, since the completion of the Rápida (VR1) and the other major (VE) highways, accessibility to all areas of the island is relatively quick and easy. Hire cars are available at the airport and from hotels and agencies in **Funchal** and around the island. Taxis are another option at reasonable cost. Drivers will take you to the start of each walk and, if required, will collect you at the end. Taxis can be hired for half or full days and drivers carry standard price lists for journeys outside **Funchal**. See Appendix A for taxi phone numbers.

Bus journeys can be an adventure and a number of the walks in this book can be accessed by public transport (see each walk introduction). Bus services vary considerably in the urban and rural areas (See Appendix E for current bus information including the website addresses for the main operators on the island). Bus routes also change frequently so it's important to check these out at the time of your visit. We recommend the latest edition of Madeira Bus & Touring Map (Published by Discovery Walking Guides Ltd), invaluable for bus users and car drivers alike. You can also get information on routes and bus numbers from your hotel or from the tourist offices and timetables can be purchased from the bus and newspaper kiosks in **Funchal**.

PLACES TO VISIT AND OTHER THINGS TO DO
The following are some of our favourites, worthy of particular mention.

GARDENS

Monte Palace Tropical Gardens
Acquired by the Barardo Foundation in 1987 these beautiful gardens occupy an area of 70,000 sq mtrs. Planted with exotic flora from around the world and with magnificent water features including waterfalls and lagoons, the entire gardens are enhanced with wonderful works of art. There are two museums; one houses a mineral and gem collection while the second displays a huge collection of Zimbabwe contemporary sculpture.

Palheiro Gardens and Quinta de Ferreiro
Bought by the Blandy wine family in the late 1800s, the **Palheiro Gardens** are famous for their diversity of plants and magnificent trees and their beautiful setting in the hills to the east of **Funchal**.

Magnolia, Palheiro Gardens

Quinta do Arco Rose Garden, Arco de São Jorge
The garden has received international recognition from the World Federation of Rose Societies; 17,000 roses and 1,450 species are on display.

Jardim Botânico da Madeira
Opened in 1960 this 80 acres garden is home to more than 2,500 plant species, 300 exotic birds and 200 species of indigenous plants. The gardens can be accessed by the *teleférico,* the one from **Babosas Square** descending directly into the *parque*.

NATURE RESERVES

Núcleo de Dragoeiros das Neves
A nature conservation centre close to **São Gonçalo**, east of **Funchal**, this reserve houses a small museum in the former farmhouse.

The gardens are dedicated to indigenous plant species of the coastal areas of Madeira including a magnificent group

Dracaena draco

of centuries old dragon trees (Dracaena draco) a Macaronesian endemic once in abundance on the island but now almost extinct, there are only two surviving naturally near **Ribeira Brava**.

Posto Florestal - Ribeiro Frio
This reserve displays a collection of endemic plants specific to the *laurisilva* and in summer, you'll find the rare yellow foxglove (Isoplexis sceptrum), Musschia wollastonii and carrot trees. It's also the site of a trout farm and fish hatchery, providing brown trout to replenish Madeira's watercourses.

NATURAL HISTORY MUSEUMS
Rota da Cal (The Lime Route)

A relatively new museum in **Lamaceiros** village, **São Vicente** and a unique site of geological and botanical importance, **Rota da Cal** is situated in a sea limestone outbreak with fossils over 5 million years old and is also an area of the *laurisilva*, attracting endemic bird species and numerous species of endemic flora.

Aquúario da Madeira Porto Moniz

Aquário da Madeira Porto Moniz

A small aquarium opened 2005 in the wonderful old **São João** fort next to the harbour in **Porto Moniz**; its interior is superb and was inspired by the surrounding marine environment.

Volcano Centre and Caves São Vicente
This cultural and learning centre focusing on Madeira's volcanic origins offers a number of daily guided tours through the **Grutas de São Vicente** caves and lava tubes, plus exhibitions and exciting film of the journey of the island. For opening times and contact details for the Gardens, Nature Reserve and Natural History Museums, please refer to Appendix B -

OTHER THINGS TO DO

A Trip to the Desertas Island
The Gavião Luxury Yacht sails to the uninhabited nature reserve of the Desertas, habitat of the endangered monk seal and rare wild life bird sanctuary. Moor in a sheltered cove of **Deserta Grande**, then go ashore to visit the guard's accommodation and the information centre. The round trip from Funchal marina

Santa Maria below Cabo Girão

takes around 7 - 8 hours and includes lunch and refreshments.

Sail on the Santa Maria (Replica of Columbus' vessel)

Daily sails leave **Funchal** harbour usually heading for **Cabo Girão**. This wonderful vessel offers the chance to see whales and dolphin, coastal sightseeing and swimming in the marvelous turquoise waters below the highest cliff.

Dolphin & Whale watching from Calheta
Take a sail on the Ilhéu, a 1946 Gaffing Ketch making 3hr daytime trips and sunset trips from the **Calheta Marina** or from **Madelena do Mar**.

Discover Funchal

Jacarandas in bloom, Funchal

Take a stroll from the famous **Reid's Palace Hotel** along the Jacaranda lined avenues. En-route you'll pass beside the Presidents residency **Quinta Vigia** and the magnificent **Santa Catarina Park** on the right, across from which is the **Dona Amélia Garden**, and lower down, the exotic **Municipal Park** in the city centre.

Palacio e Fortaleza de São Lourenço

This short walk takes you past the wonderful **Palácio e Fortaleza de São Lourenço** and the famous **Golden Gate Café** before arriving at the **Sé Cathedral** (built 1485 -1514), one of Madeira's oldest buildings.

Visit Funchal's Zona Velha (Old Town)

Pavement cafés in Zona Velha

Visit the famous and colourful produce market, then wander along **Rua D. Carlos** with its pretty pavement restaurants and lovely chapel, before arriving at the **São Trigo Fortress** housing a modern art gallery and a wonderful restaurant.

Return along **Rua Santa Maria** a quaint street bustling with restaurants and enjoy the **Arte de Portas Abertas** exhibition (Art of Open Doors); a project designed to involve local artists in the regeneration of the area.

Santa Cruz beach

Arte de Portas Abertas

Coastal Resorts

Visit the towns of **Santo Cruz**, **Machico** and **Porto da Cruz** or take a drive along the stunning north coast to **Porto Moniz**. A visit to many of these towns can be linked to the walks starting or ending close to these areas.

Take a cable car ride (the *Teleférico*)
There are now seven operating around the island serving the following areas: -

- **Funchal**, sea front to **Monte**
- **Babosas** to the **Botanical Gardens**
- **Garajau** to the beachside complex - (besides the impressive statue of Christ, a replica of the Rio statue)

Cristo Rei

The Teleférico to Rocha do Navio Nature Reserve

- **Achada da Cruz** to the *fajás* and vineyards at beach level
- **Rancho**, **Câmara de Lobos**, to the agricultural areas at sea level
- **Rocha do Navio**, **Santana** to the vineyards and islets along the coast
- **Fajá dos Padros**

Fajã dos Padres

The latter cable car takes you down to **Fajá dos Padros** at **Cabo Girão**, for sun, sea, food and wine and a fantastic place to wander around cobbled pathways to the cottages, vineyards and orchards.

São Trigo Fortress

Visit Fortim do Faial
This is a small mock fort complete with 10 cannons (built between the 18th and 19th century) is really a lookout point or monument built by the Catanho de Maneses family commanding wonderful views along the north coast over **Faial**, **Porto da Cruz** and **Eagle Rock**.

Cannons at the lookout, Faial

Cabo Girão Sky Walk
Why not take a bus or taxi up to the new Skywalk at **Cabo Girão**, one of Madeira's most popular attractions. The platform is constructed of transparent glass providing stunning views down the sea cliffs; it's quite an exhilarating experience.

Information and contact details for other activities including sailing, whale and dolphin watching, bird watching and canyoning are given in Appendix B.

View through the Skywalk's floor

SYMBOLS RATING GUIDE

DWG's Symbols Rating Bar shows key information about a walking route in a quick glance. Remember that effort/exertion and refreshment ratings are the author's opinion and the time shown is walking time without stops.

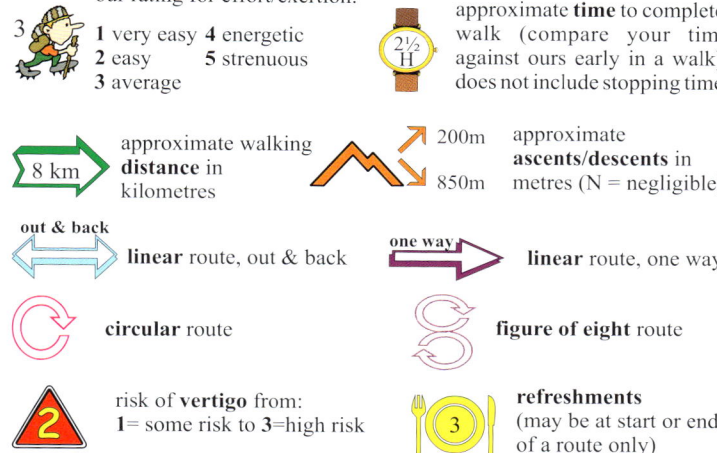

our rating for effort/exertion:
1 very easy **4** energetic
2 easy **5** strenuous
3 average

approximate **time** to complete a walk (compare your times against ours early in a walk) - does not include stopping time

approximate walking **distance** in kilometres

200m / 850m approximate **ascents/descents** in metres (N = negligible)

linear route, out & back

linear route, one way

circular route

figure of eight route

risk of **vertigo** from:
1= some risk to 3=high risk

refreshments
(may be at start or end of a route only)

Notes on the text

Place names are shown in **bold text**, except where we refer to a written sign, when they are enclosed in single quotation marks. Local or unusual words are shown in *italics*, and are explained in the accompanying text.

Walk descriptions include:

- timing in minutes, shown as (40M)
- compass directions, shown as (NW)
- heights in metres, shown as (1355m)
- GPS waypoints, shown as (Wp.3)

A Note About Walking Times

Walking times create more discussion than any other aspect of walking guide books. Our walking times are for ***continuous walking*** at an easy pace without stops, representing the quickest time you are likely to complete a route. Most of us walk at a similar pace; approx 4-6kmh. As our routes are planned as fun adventures you are unlikely to simply march along the route from start to finish. We all take stops to enjoy the views, marvel at the flora, or simply to take a break. As a result, our time will be longer than the 'continuous walking' time and we suggest you add 25-50% to those times, to allow for the stops you'll make along the route.

WALK LOCATOR MAP

MAP PROVENANCE

Simplified and adapted map data provided by **Discovery Walking Guides Ltd.** (copyright David Brawn) has been used to prepare this locator map.

The latest editions of **Madeira Tour & Trail Map** and **Madeira Bus & Touring Map** are available from booksellers.

Digital mapping for a variety of destinations including Madeira is available from:
www.dwgwalking.co.uk

Please Note:

This locator map is intended to give a general indication of each walk area.

WALK LOCATOR MAP

EUROPE

THE MADEIRA ARCHIPELAGO

MADEIRA ISLAND   PORTO SANTO

DESERTAS ISLANDS

SELVAGENS ISLANDS

AFRICA

Madeira Walks 1

MAP NOTES AND LEGEND

The map sections in this book have been adapted from **Madeira Tour & Trail Map** published by **Discovery Walking Guides Ltd.**

Madeira Tour & Trail Map and **Madeira Bus & Touring Map**, are available from booksellers.

Madeira Tour & Trail Legend

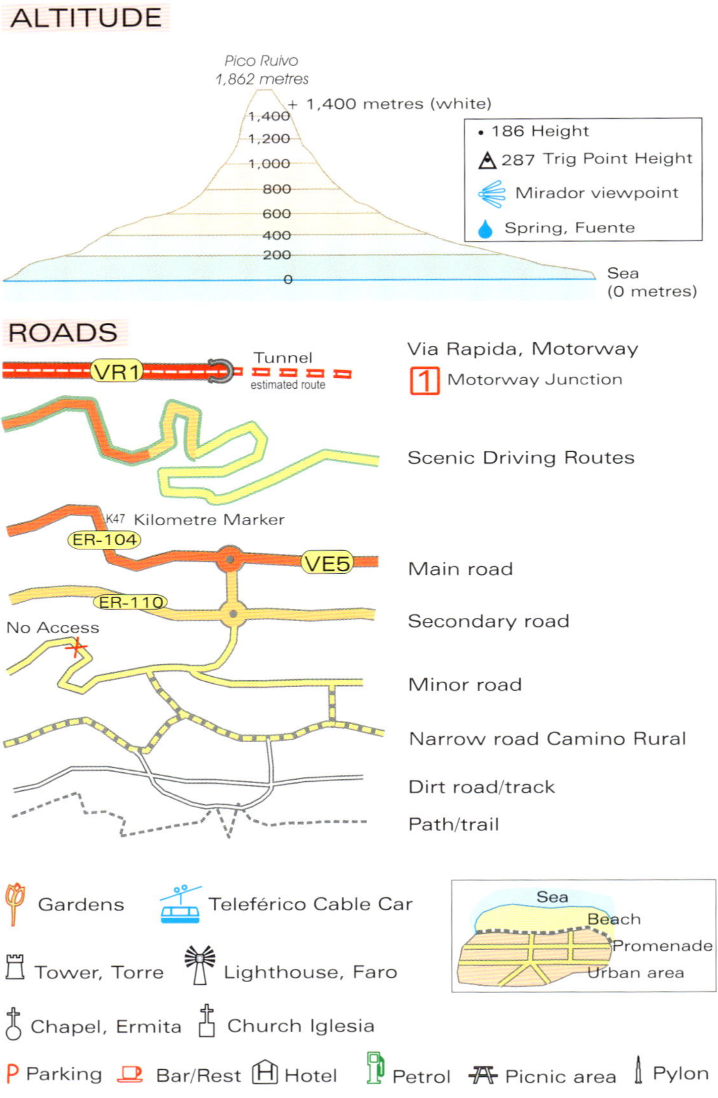

ALTITUDE

Pico Ruivo
1,862 metres

+ 1,400 metres (white)
1,400
1,200
1,000
800
600
400
200
0

Sea (0 metres)

- • 186 Height
- ▲ 287 Trig Point Height
- Mirador viewpoint
- Spring, Fuente

ROADS

- VR1 — Via Rapida, Motorway
- Tunnel estimated route
- 1 Motorway Junction
- Scenic Driving Routes
- K47 Kilometre Marker
- ER-104 / VE5 Main road
- ER-110 Secondary road
- No Access
- Minor road
- Narrow road Camino Rural
- Dirt road/track
- Path/trail

Gardens Teleférico Cable Car

Tower, Torre Lighthouse, Faro

Chapel, Ermita Church Iglesia

P Parking Bar/Rest Hotel Petrol Picnic area Pylon

Sea / Beach / Promenade / Urban area

USING GPS ON MADEIRA

All the routes in our Madeira books have been recorded by gps and are accurately described, so adventuring on our routes is simply a matter of following the walk description.

A gps is not necessary but is very useful if you want to know exactly where you are on a walking route. If it's your first time on Madeira then a gps will be useful in finding the start of each walking route; with the walking route's waypoints loaded in your gps, simply activate the 'Go To' function for Waypoint 1.

All the waypoints for our Madeira walking routes are available as a free downloadable zip file. Locate the download page on our website, then download the zip file to your hard drive, unzip the file and you will have all the individual waypoint files in gpx file format; then simply load the files you want into your gps or phone app.

If you are thinking of a gps for your walking navigation, then our **GPS The Easy Way** introduction to gps walking navigation is available as a free download in pdf format from DWG's website:- www.dwgwalking.co.uk

3G phone users should look at the gps apps by **MyTrails** and **Viewranger** who supply digital editions of our Tour & Trail Maps for their apps which enables you to use your phone offline as a full mapping gps unit without incurring any phone call or roaming charges. For more information see their websites.

Discovery Walking Guides publish Custom Map digital editions of Tour & Trail Maps in kmz file format for use in Google Earth and with the Custom Maps function of Garmin mapping gps units such as eTrex20/30, Oregon, Dakota, Montana. See DWG's website:- www.dwgwalking.co.uk for information.

1 PRAIA FORMOSA to CÂMARA DE LOBOS

The fishing village of **Câmara de Lobos** is our destination for this easy route along a promenade linking the hotel/lido area with this pretty parish. It takes its name from the time when the seas around the island supported a great number of monk seals; the Portuguese named these sea wolves (*lobos marinhos*). Regrettably, today the seals are infrequent visitors to the shores, except for a colony inhabiting the **Ilhas Desertas (Desertas Islands)**.

Looking across the harbour

The best way to see the village is on foot, following our route along quaint streets, beside wonderful old buildings and to the stunning harbour with its beached boats. No wonder Winston Churchill fell in love with this charming place and captured the views in his famous paintings.

Though this is a linear one-way route, you could easily make it into a pleasant circular by returning via the hop-on hop-off service of the sightseeing bus. It operates throughout the day between **Funchal** and **Câmara de Lobos**, passing through **Praia Formosa**. Details for the yellow sight-seeing bus are given at the end of the walking notes.

* if walking the route one way;
if walking there and back to the start, double these times and distances

Access by hire car or taxi: Follow **Estrada Monumental** (ER229) to the **Praia Formosa** junction at the western end of the hotel/lido area. Parking is available at the **Praia** car park.

Access by bus: Town buses Nºs 1, 24 & 43, plus numerous Rodoeste buses provide a frequent service between Funchal and **Câmara de Lobos** all

24 Madeira Walks 1

passing through the *lido* area and **Praia Formosa**.

From the **Estrada Monumental** junction (Wp.1), we drop down the road passing under the bridge and taking a right turn, arrive at the **Praia** car park beside the promenade (Wp.2 0M). Going right on the new railed section of promenade, we pass through the pretty **Praia Restaurant** and bar to continue along the walkway as it contours around the sea cliffs. Long sections of the promenade have been constructed on concrete pillars and from time to time we can feel the sway as we walk along. Passing the **Hotel Orca Praia** (amusingly translated as killer whale beach) we meander along enjoying the blue sea and sky and the rolling waves by our side.

After passing the Madeira Cement plant (fortunately the only blot on the landscape) the promenade leaves the beach (Wp.3 25M) along a pillared ramp taking us towards the ER229. Almost at the road and with a left turn access down to a dry dock (Wp.4 30M), we follow a pedestrian pathway running parallel with the road. This is walled and signed, the route well manicured as it drops down towards **Câmara de Lobos**, passing beside some amazing ochre coloured cliffs en-route.

Our first stunning view of the harbour

Rounding a right hand bend, we come across the first stunning view of the fishing village; from hereon, it just gets better and better!

Quaint houses appear and we pass beside an ancient limekiln as we descend through this old part of the town (Wp.5 35M).

The limekiln

Rounding another right hand bend a panoramic view of the parish, the harbour and the beaching area crammed with multi-coloured boats, opens up before us; it's quite breathtaking.

Multi-coloured boats

Passing buildings on our right, one of which was used by Winston Churchill for his famous paintings (Wp.6 45M), we drop down steps beside the houses to arrive on the roadway behind the beached boats.

Turning left (Wp.7 50M), we pass beside numerous pavement cafes, a lovely spot to take refreshments and soak up the atmosphere.

Here you can try the typical *Poncha* drink or nibble some salted, dried 'she-cat', a speciality of **Câmara de Lobos**, a dogfish-like shark caught in the seas off Madeira and left to dry. You'll see these skins hanging from the nearby fishing boats.

She-cat skins; drying

The harbour lies a few metres below, where we turn right passing beside the pretty chapel of **Capela de Nossa Senhora da Conceição**, and then continue around the harbour wall before reaching a stairway on our right below the towering rock and lighthouse (Wp.8 55M).

Largo da República

Climbing the steps the route now follows a higher-level promenade before reaching **Largo da República** on top of the sea cliffs (Wp.9 70M). Here we find a few places to eat, the **Coral** being an excellent seafood restaurant; there's also the bandstand and the lovely church of **São Sebastião**, dating back to 1426.

Passing between the restaurant and the church, we emerge onto a charming cobbled street **Rua São João de Deus** with pavement cafés and lots of flowering tubs and baskets.

Rua São João de Deus

The street ends in **Largo do Poço** where we turn right along **Rua Nossa Senhora da Conceição** to drop back down to our finish in the harbour, from where our alternatives are to retrace our steps back to the starting point, or return by bus, though it's well worth the walk back as we take in a completely different perspective, this time of the hotel district along the cliffs on the approach to **Funchal**. Add a further 1¼ hours if you're walking the return route.

Yellow Sight Seeing Bus - Funchal/Cãmara de Lobos
This frequent daily service (except Christmas Day) between **Funchal** and **Cãmara de Lobos** calls at many other destinations in and around **Funchal**.Tickets are for a hop-on - hop-off service over a 48 hr period and cost €10.80 adults and €6 children aged 4-10. Buy Yellow tickets on board or via the internet at www.yellowbustours.com, also from the Tourist Office **Avenida do Mar** and a kiosk close to the **Monumental Lido Hotel.**

2 ROMEIROS TO JASMIN TEA ROOMS & PALHEIRO GARDENS

Palheiro Gardens and Quinta do Ferreiro

Levada dos Tornos runs at 600m above sea level, linking the settlements of **Monte** and **Camacha**. This trail takes in a central section between **Romeiros** and the **Palheiro Estate** and combines the *levada* walk with a visit to the Jasmin Tea House, ending in the beautiful **Palheiro Gardens**.

We believe this will be an extremely popular choice, particularly for those staying in and around **Funchal**, and we suggest you make it into a whole day circular outing with the use of the excellent bus service.

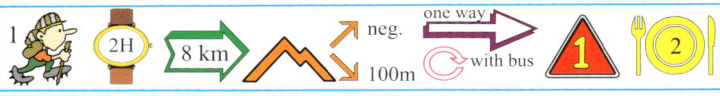

*circular with bus service

Access by car or taxi: leave the VR1 at Junction 13 and follow the signs for the **Botanical Gardens** and the **Choupana Hills Hotel**. **Romeiros** village is situated around 1 km from the hotel.

Access by bus: Horários provide a frequent and regular service from **Funchal** to **Romeiros** on bus N°29. There are frequent direct returns from **Palheiro Gardens** to **Funchal** on bus N°s 36A and 37, or from the ER205 below the tea house on bus N°47.

From the **Romeiros** bus stop we take concrete steps and a cobbled path towards the village where we head to the signpost for 'Levada dos Tornos' (Wp.1 0M). Fifteen metres along, we take a short flight of steps on the left to reach the channel. Turning right, we almost immediately reach a watercourse where we take steps up and then down, onto the l*evada*.

The forest along most of the trail is predominantly pine, eucalyptus and acacia, the broad *levada* path lined with a profusion of wild flowers including many species of Fabaceae (Pea), as well as lovely displays of Greater Periwinkle, (Vinca major), Red Flowering Sorrel (Oxalis purpurea), Red Valerian, Scarlet Pimpernel and the large white Calla Lilies (Calla aethiopica), all in season of

Greater Periwinkle (Vinca major)

course. Along short sections the colourful countryside changes, as we follow the water channel into side valleys where the old dark forest envelopes us. The first is steep where we cross the ravine's black rock water runoff. Out of the valley, we turn into a second pocket of old forest, crossing a hand railed bridge over a stream (Wp.2 20M) followed by a steel section of railings. Passing caves in the cliff on our left, we come to a section where the *levada* has been straightened and broad steps cross it above a bus stop on the road below us. Curving left, this idyllic path is rudely interrupted as we reach a gate. being the entrance to the **Choupana Hills Complex** (Wp.3). Note: this hotel was closed in 2016 due to severe fire damage to the main buildings. However the pathway through the wooden chalets (which were mostly untouched by the fires) is still open for public access.

Crossing over the private road, we continue through the gardens along a 'public right of way' path, and after passing beside the hotel lodges, we leave the resort through another gate crossing the *levada*. Here a huge retaining wall appears on our left, behind which loom the hotel buildings. Emerging onto a road where the channel is tunneled underneath, we cross to pick up the levada again (Wp.4 40M). Continuing our stroll, we soon pass beside a levada water house and water change point (Wp.5 45M), shortly before crossing a steep tarmac lane. Passing a patch of houses which contrast with the meadow landscape, we have good views over **Funchal**, as we cross over a road bridging the channel.

The waterhouse

A few minutes ahead, after passing **Horténsia Tea Rooms** in the **Quinta Gorick** estate - an alternative option for a rest and

refreshments (Wp.6 65M) - our path continues along a quiet stretch of forest through dappled sunlight and tunnels of mimosa, before arriving on the regional ER201. Crossing over, we continue to follow the channel on the opposite side through the woodland. A short section 50 metres along needs careful footwork, before we arrive at a sign beside the *levada* directing us right down a narrow pathway into the gardens of **Jasmin Tea House** (Wp.7 85M). Reopened in July 2014, the tea house offers a range of light meals, delicious home made cakes and specialist teas and you are guaranteed a very warm welcome by Nick and Sam the owners. The tea house is open daily (except Mondays) between 10.00 a.m and 5.00 pm.

Refreshed and back on our trail, the channel contours the hillside and there are views of **Funchal** along this section. We reach the ER205 (Wp.8 95M), picking up the *levada* on the opposite side and three minutes along, emerge onto a road with a warehouse to our right (Wp.9 110M). At this point we leave the *levada* going right to drop down the tarred road. This bends to the left 150 metres along, before reaching a T-junction in front of the wall of a reservoir. **Palheiro Gardens** are signed to the right. Following right, passing restaurant **O Palheiro**, we descend this leafy lane, the boundary wall of **Palheiro** now on our left, to arrive at the gate of the estate (Wp.10 120M).

The bus stop for your return to **Funchal** is directly opposite the gate, but if you find after your visit to the gardens, that you've just missed a bus, you can turn left walking 500 metres along the road, going right at a fork, to arrive on the ER205. The bus stop is on the left at the junction and all buses stopping here will take you back to **Funchal**.

The Palheiro Estate
The famous Blandy family, the original English settlers and wine merchants from the Victorian era, own the **Palheiro Estate**, including the wonderful gardens and golf course. In the centre of the estate you'll find the striking **Quinta do Ferreiro**

The protea garden

The topiary garden

surrounded by the main garden, the sunken garden and the chapel (*capela*). Close to the lovely hotel at the bottom of the estate you'll also find the **Casa da Chá** offering lunches and refreshments in a lovely setting of vernacular architecture.

The gardens are open daily (except Christmas Day and New Year's Day) from 9.00 a.m. to 5.30 p.m. Admission is €10.50 for adults, children are free. Further information can be found on www.palheiroestate.com.

3 LEVADA DO NORTE AND LEVADA DAS RABAÇAS - ENCUMEADA

Boca da Encumeada (1007m) sits at the head of a great rift, dividing the island at an almost central point. The highest peaks lie to the east with the plateau of **Paúl da Serra** to the west. From the viewpoint on the summit, both north and south coastlines are visible; it's best to go there in the morning as later in the day blankets of cloud can drape the summit obliterating these stunning views.

The view east to Pico Grande

The ER105 regional highway climbing from **Ribeira Brava** and over the **Encumeada Pass**, as well as the ER228 which drops down into **São Vicente**, are two of the most scenic routes on the island, making **Boca da Encumeada** a vibrant centre for tourists and hikers.

Our short trail follows **Levada do Norte** and **Levada das Rabaças** along the southern mountain slopes above **Ribeira Brava**, the pathway, bordered with exotic flora, allowing stunning views along its whole length.

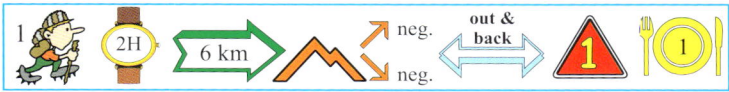

Access by hire car or taxi:
Take the VE4 north from **Ribeira Brava**, turning left on the ER105 for **Serra da Agua** and **Encumeada**. **Snack Bar Encumeada** is located on the right of the road as you approach the summit. From the west, approach via the **Paúl da Serra** crossroads, taking the ER105 east for 12 kms through **Encumeada** pass and turning right after the gift shop signed 'Ribeira Brava'. The snack bar is located a few metres below the junction.

Access by bus:
Rodoeste provide infrequent services on routes Nºs 6 and 139 from **Funchal** and **Ribeira Brava** to **Boca da Encumeada**.

(Note: most journeys on both buses go via **Encumeada** but occasionally may be routed along the VE4 via **Túnel Encumeada**, so make sure to check with the Tourist Office or the bus kiosks before embarking.)

Setting off

Across from the **Encumeada Snack Bar** a short flight of steps lead us up to an information panel on the shoulder of **Levada do Norte** (Wp.1 0M). This indicates the route for the **PR17 Caminho do Pináculo e Folhadal**, which we follow for a short distance before heading off onto **Levada das Rabaças**.

Following the channel upstream along a substantial path, our route is bordered with Agapanthus (Lily of the Nile) and Hydrangea. Soon we pass beside the water keeper's house, a pretty building surrounded by lush vegetation; a water separation point is negotiated a little further ahead.

Splendid views open up along the route looking down on the **Ribeira Brava** valley and east to **Pico Grande**, soon after arriving at a *miradouro* (Wp.2 18M) from where the **Residencial Encumeada Hotel** is seen nestling on the slopes below us.

The tunnel at Wp.3

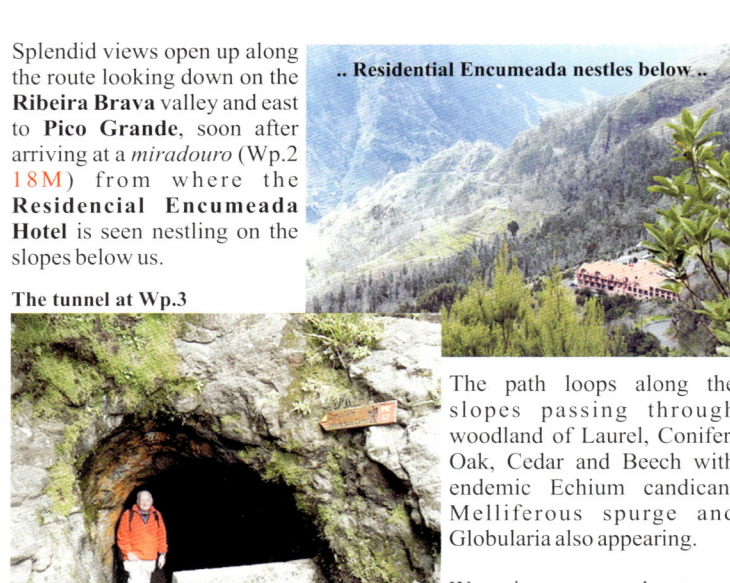

.. Residential Encumeada nestles below ..

The path loops along the slopes passing through woodland of Laurel, Conifer, Oak, Cedar and Beech with endemic Echium candican, Melliferous spurge and Globularia also appearing.

We arrive at a tunnel entrance on our right (Wp.3 20M)

where our trail leaves the PR17 route, the latter heading off through the tunnel. Our route continues ahead following **Levada das Rabaças**, the vegetation soon thinning out, opening up vistas all around. South is **Serra da Água** and ahead, magnificent peaks appear.

As the peaks tower ahead of us, a few narrow sections of channel follow which are mildly precipitous, before we arrive at a large valley head with waterfalls to our right.

Approaching the end of the route

Arriving at a tunnel entrance (Wp.4 55M) the walk comes to an end and from here we retrace our steps back to the starting point, enjoying the different perspective of the return journey (Wp.1 110M).

The bus stop to return to your base can be found a few metres below the **Encumeada Snack Bar** on the left of the ER105. Note that this stop is for both directions.

Extension (Total route 12 kms - 4 hrs one way)
Levada das Rabaças enters the tunnel at Wp4 making a continuous route to **Cascalho** where the trail then links with Walk 29. (See note on walk 29 for details.)

Please note that this continuous route remains impassable at the time of our update (November 2018) but hopefully may reopen at some point in the future. However it is essential that anyone wishing to walk on to **Cristo Rio** should <u>always</u> check the status of the route with the tourist office or with the *Lavadeiros* at the **Encumeada Water House** before setting out.

4 LEVADA DO NORTE - ESTREITO DE CÂMARA DE LOBOS to CABO GIRÃO

Cabo Girão is the second highest sea cliff in Europe, rising 580m above sea level. In 2012 the renewed belvedere and skywalk were opened to the public and this amazing viewpoint is now claimed to be one of Madeira's most popular tourist attractions with an estimated 1800 visitors per day.

Similar to the one in America's Grand Canyon, the skywalk is constructed of transparent glass to provide stunning views down the sea cliffs into the ocean below. From the belvedere we also have panoramic views across from **Estreito de Câmara de Lobos** to **Funchal Bay**.

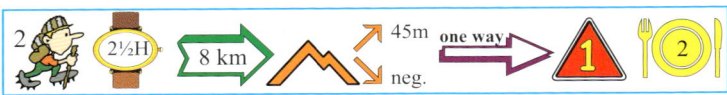

Access by car or taxi:
Follow the ER229 to the centre of **Estreito de Câmara de Lobos**, turning left immediately after the church signed 'Jardim da Serra'. The *levada* crosses over the road approximately 600m ahead.

Access by bus:
Rodoeste provide a frequent service from **Funchal** to **Estreito de Câmara de Lobos** and on to **Ribeira Brava** via **Cruz da Caldeira** close to **Cabo Girão**. Selected services also go direct to and from the **Belvedere**.

For the outward route to the start of the *levada*, take bus N°96 alighting at the **Levada do Norte** bus stop just above the centre of **Estreito**. Return from the **Belvedere** or from **Cruz da Caldeira** bus stop which is 700 m along the road from the viewpoint on the ER229 taking any bus traveling east via **Estreito de Câmara do Lobos** to **Funchal** or west to **Ribeira Brava**.

The start of the walk

We pick up the *levada* on the left side of the road where a large sign 'Levada do Norte' directs us along a pink paved pathway under the vines (Wp.1 0M). Soon crossing a small bridge at a valley head then passing beside more houses and agricultural plots, we meet a tarred road where the channel is culverted; it is picked up again around 300m ahead.

With houses and vineyards scattered across the hillside, the trail heads into a deeply wooded valley where after twenty minutes walking, the *levada* suddenly sweeps to the right (Wp.2 20M). Here the concrete shoulder becomes extremely narrow passing under overhanging rock, so our route follows a detour below the channel rejoining it again a short distance ahead.

Entering the deep valley

This beautiful valley which is rich in flora, is extremely deep and once again the *levada* becomes precipitous where rocks overhang the channel. Here it is again necessary to take the detour path below the water channel to avoid this short section. Nevertheless, easy walking follows and a short distance ahead we cross a bridge over a deep gorge, the river tumbling down waterfalls on our right before dropping into the gorge below (Wp.3 35M).

Now circling below the settlements of **Jardim da Serra** we arrive at a second river where a new iron bridge has been erected (Wp.4 50M). Crossing over, our route heads out of the valley towards the village of **Garachico**.

Along the next section we have wonderful views across the coastline and over to the **Desertas Islands** with the vast patchwork of vineyards stretching out before us down the deep valley.

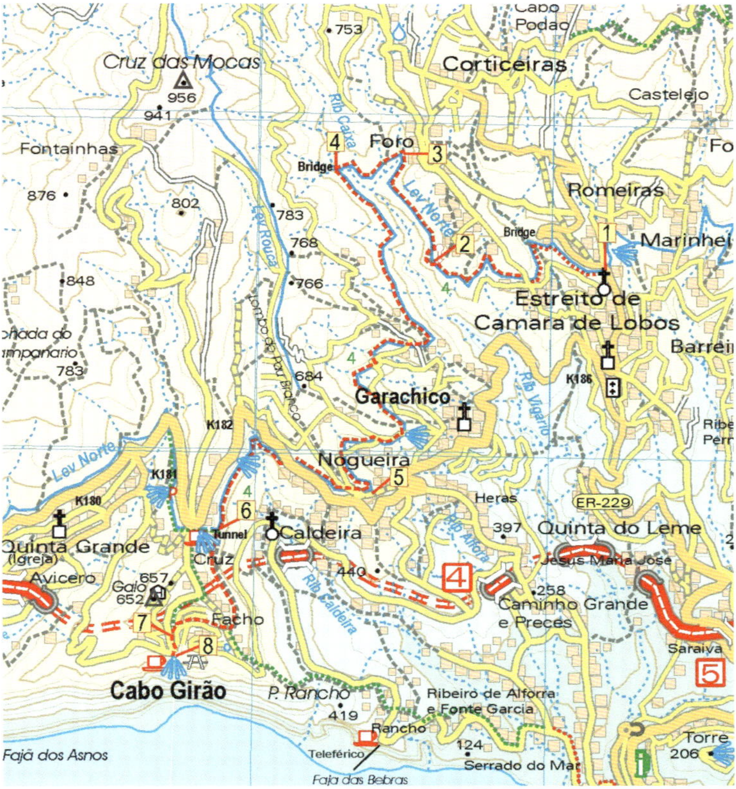

We arrive at a new road and roundabout and leave the levada climbing steps to pick up the channel again on the right of the road after the bend. The *levada* maintains height along this next section, where it is mostly covered as it passes between rural houses for around 25 minutes before emerging onto a newly constructed section. We pass beside a wall and a *levada* tunnel on our right and continue to where the channel reaches a dead end. Taking a sloping path on the left, the route descends to a water tank where we go right up a stepped lane to meet the *levada* again on the opposite side (Wp.5 105M).

A few minutes ahead, the channel disappears as we cross a pretty area of trees and undergrowth where in the past, a landslide obliterated the channel. We arrive at a waterfall at the valley head and continue along the western edge of the valley where the next section of channel has been rebuilt. Soon after the *levada* makes a right turn to enter a tunnel (Wp.6 125M) approximately 300m long, leading to the far side of **Gabo Girão**.

View east to Câmara de Lobos and Funchal

We leave **Levada do Norte** at this point, now continuing straight ahead to follow the smaller *levada* signed 'Vereda Levada do Facho'. We're now passing through the settlement of **Nogueira**, the road from the Holiday Property Bond Timeshare Complex seen below us on our left.

Around ten minutes after crossing over a steep stepped pathway, **Levada do Facho** comes to an end and here steps lead up right to join the road in the HPB complex (Wp.7 140M). Turning right, our route now ascends the road between the reception building and apartment blocks to reach the **Cabo Girão** belvedere and the amazing skywalk (Wp.8 150M).

The skywalk

After enjoying the views and the atmosphere at this spectacular cliff top, we can either retrace our steps back to the starting point, or take a taxi or bus back to base.

There's a taxi stand in the car park behind the belvedere (a taxi will cost around €15 back to the start of the walk above **Estreito**. For bus users follow the viewpoint road to its junction with the ER229 in **Cruz de Caldeira**, taking any bus east via **Estreito** to **Funchal** or any west to **Ribeira Brava**.

5 LEVADA DO PIORNAIS - MADEIRA SHOPPING TO FUNCHAL LIDO AREA

The **Socorridos Valley** is our destination for this varied trail along **Levada dos Piornais**, locally referred to as the 'city' *levada*. The route negotiates a series of spectacular tunnels along the valley wall, shortly before reaching the magnificent winged bridge on the **Via Rápida**. This 'must do' route provides a wonderful introduction to the delights of Madeira walking, although sure-footedness and a head for heights are essential. This one-way trail can be undertaken in either direction and combined with the excellent bus service, it's easy to return to your starting point.

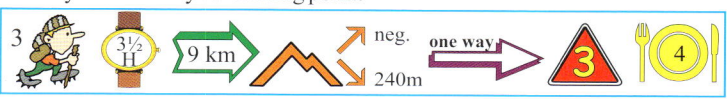

Access by hire car or taxi: Madeira Shopping car park entrance, beside the tower advertising 'Burger King'.

Access by bus: town buses N°s 8, 16 & 50 to **Madeira Shopping**.

At the road junction just below **Madeira Shopping** (Wp.1 2M) we turn right onto **Travessa do Tanque**, a minor road running between two commercial buildings, **Levada do Curral** flowing on our right. A short distance ahead, after house Nº97, the road turns left; we follow the *levada* right to loop around a shallow valley. Reaching another tarred road, we cross over to the opposite side and continue down a narrow path between a banana plantation and the first house (Wp.2 10M). Our path becomes a narrow lane, the **Travessa do Pinheiro das Voltas,** bordered by pretty houses, as we continue down to reach a crossroad with the **Pinheiro das Voltas** regional road (Wp.3 20M).

Turning right in front of a snack bar, we head down the road for around 350 metres before picking up a concrete track leading off to the right (Wp.4 28M). Following this to its end at a house, we go down a series of stone steps leading off to our left (Wp.5 30M). The steps descend 60 metres to arrive on the shoulder of **Levada dos Piornais** (Wp.6 38M), high above the industrial complex where we're treated to an impressive exhibition of water engineering with tunnel sections.

Negotiating the aqueduct

The channel flows across an aqueduct but appears to be built on thin air, the short tunnels linked by seemingly impossible sections of *levada* (all railed). To negotiate these we must crouch and crawl under the low arches; once through, the excitement and exhilaration will make you want to go back and do it all over again.

If you doubt your ability to traverse the tunnels, then take the alternative concrete steps at either end of the tunnel section to descend the valley and ascend at the opposite end (Wp.7 48M). Take your choice, but, if you've come this far and can do the tunnels, you won't forget the experience. Following the channel, it's less than one kilometre before we arrive at an information panel above the **Via Rápida**, just east of the winged bridge, a spectacular sight from this elevation (Wp.8 52M). We cross over a narrow road to pick up the *levada* again in front of house Nº526 and continue through a banana plantation bordered on our left by houses.

The winged bridge on Via Rápida

Entering the tunnel sections

From this point the *levada* is covered over as it sweeps around the plantation, crossing a local access road around mid-point. Though close to the city, this is an attractive area; mountains come into view and the *levada* is dotted with neat houses and gardens along most of its length. A short distance after crossing the access road, we pass house Nº400 and reach steps off to our left, climbing between houses (Wp.9 75M), while we continue to follow the *levada*.

On this level path, it takes only a few minutes to reach the regional road in **Santa Rita** (Wp.10 82M) where the channel disappears, now piped under the roads in this developed area.

We turn left to head up the main street passing **Rápida** slip roads on our right and the road up to the church and **Bar Santa Rita** on our left, the latter a pleasant half-way point to stop for refreshment. Continuing on the main street, we reach a roundabout (Wp.11 85M). There's no pedestrian footpath along this short section of road, so care is needed. Turning right onto **Rua Arriero**, we pass under the **Rápida** bridge and turn right to cross over the slip road where our route drops down steps beside the driveway of the Dilectus Assisted Residence building. The *levada* is covered along this section as it passes under the complex and then follows alongside a high stone wall to arrive at a building with gates, where we turn right and then left to follow the path again.

... pretty gardens ...

We arrive at a house where we descend cobbled steps to reach a lane; turning left, we meet the *levada* again on our right for a short section before steps lead us up to the road, and crossing over, we pick up the channel on the opposite side (Wp.13 95M). Our route veers off left as we pass between older properties with pretty gardens and agricultural plots, the channel now deep and fast flowing. We have good views of the coastline and the massive sea cliff of **Cabo Girão**. Here the *levada* belongs to a rural world, quite different to that of the housing areas close by and the crowded hotel district below us.

Another twenty-five minutes along, we pass under a pretty stone arch, then over a road ascending from **Estrada Monumental**, soon followed by a bridge at a small valley head - the impressive **São Martinho** church now in view to our left (Wp.14 120M). The *levada* enters a tunnel (around 100 metres long though a torch isn't needed), taking us under a new road network. Emerging, we reach **Amparo** where the *levada* disappears under a concrete drive, we cross over to connect with the channel at **A Casa da Levada** bar (Wp.15 130M). The scene suddenly changes as we move away from the rural areas - now passing beside the **Da Cruz** hillside on our left with striking villas appearing on our right as we look down over the distinctive rooftops of **Forum Shopping Centre**.

Funchal and its harbour come into view, shortly before we arrive in **Casa Branca** to reach the end of the *levada* (Wp.16 185M). The football stadium can be seen straight ahead of us. Taking steps up to the road we turn first right down a narrow lane, **Ladeira da Casa Branca**; it's a delightful area passing between impressive houses and walled gardens albeit quite busy with traffic. The lane ends at a T-junction with a wider road; going right, we follow this until the road heads off right where we take a downhill route left. Passing more *quintas* and hotels, this road again heads off right, while we descend **Travessa do Valente** to reach **Estrada Monumental** (ER229) beside the **Hole in One** restaurant and bar (Wp.17 210M).

There are frequent bus stops along **Estrada Monumental** and a taxi stand can be found along the road a short distance to the right, close to **Hotel Monumental**.

6 LEVADA DO PIORNAIS - MADEIRA SHOPPING - SANTA RITA - CIRCULAR

This is a shorter circular option of Walk 5, still taking in **Levada dos Piornais** and its spectacular tunnels, but returning to Madeira shopping via a pretty ancient trail through banana plantations.

For access by hire car, taxi or town bus, please refer to the information given for Walk 5.

For this alternative, follow the Walk 5 from **Madeira Shopping** (from Wp.1 - Wp.9 75M) then turn left, climbing the steps passing house Nº398 on the right. Still climbing and three minutes ahead, we reach a yellow house Nº398a and walk directly in front of the pretty patio area.

Traversing the tunnels

The narrow concrete path turns left immediately after the house and continues into the plantation turning right a few metres ahead. Here the path has been covered over with a small landslip, so we need to make our way along the earthen path in the plantation for a few metres. Reaching another old property, this one possibly abandoned, we pass directly between the front doors and the traditional seating on the right (Wp.10 80M). The route turns left again and continues through the plantation soon reaching a stairway. There are around 100 steps and at the top the path continues for a few metres before squeezing between houses and the banana plantations.

This pathway is **Travessa de Santa Rita**, and is signed just after the point where the path meets a tarred road (Wp.11 90M). Ignoring the right-hand turn, we continue to climb, two minutes later reaching a road junction (Wp.12 92M). Turning left, then following a right hand bend, we continue on this wider road to a junction - we're now back at the snack bar at **Pinheira das Voltas** rejoining our outward route (Wp.3 95M). Following this in reverse, we retrace our steps on this final section to return to **Madeira Shopping** below the bus stops and taxi stand (Wp.1 120M).

7 EIRA DO SERRADO TO CURRAL DAS FREIRAS (NUN'S VALLEY)

Curral das Freiras is a traditional rural settlement, founded in the 16th Century by nuns of the Convent of Santo Clara who fled from **Funchal** following an attack by pirates in 1566 and sought permanent refuge there. The land was given over to the sisters who erected the first church in the area and created the agricultural environment, which still remains today.

The village's thriving centre relies mainly on tourism: each November it hosts a Chestnut Festival which draws in tourists and local people from across the island; displays in the cultural and traditional customs of the village are staged, while throughout the festival and during the whole year you'll find chestnut soup, chestnut bread and cakes and chestnut liquor on the menus.

Southern view from Eira do Serrado

This short trail begins at **Eira do Serrado** which sits on an impressive ridge high above the valley of **Curral** offering stunning views in all directions. The **Estalagem** offers accommodation, a restaurant and bar and a large, well-stocked souvenir shop; there's also an amazing *miradouro* only five minutes walk away.

Looking down to Curral das Freiras

The walk follows an ancient cobbled trail which originally connected **Nun's Valley** to **Funchal** and the south, before the creation of roads in the late 1950s. The path descends 400 metres making easy bends down the mountainside, providing a most spectacular approach into the valley below.

Before embarking on the walk it's well worth spending a little time at this stunning location and in particular visiting the *miradouro* which is reached along a well-manicured path leading from the hotel; the views of the central mountain range are amazing, with the majestic mountains encircling the little village of **Curral** far below.

    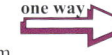

Access by hire car or taxi: leave **Funchal** via **São Martinho** heading for **Pico dos Barcelos**. Continue on the ER107 for around 10 kilometres, eventually meeting the new road and tunnel which descends into the **Curral** valley. For the start of the walk, turn left before the tunnel entrance, signed 'Eira do Serrado', parking at the **Estalagem** car park.

Access by bus:
Horário bus N°81 operates a frequent service between **Funchal** and **Curral das Freiras** as far as **Lombo Chão** and also serves **Eira do Serrado**.(Note: not all services go down the final section to reach the hotel at **Eira do Serrada** so we advise that you check the route before leaving.)

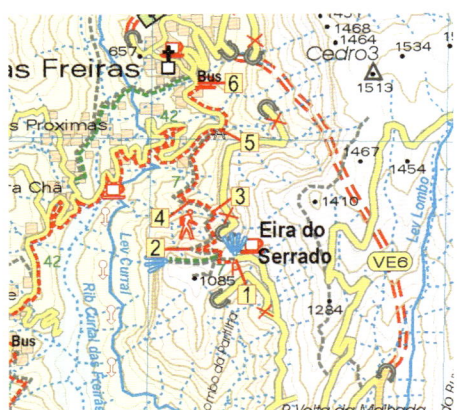

Heading for the point where the road enters the hotel car park, we descend a flight of steps leading down behind the building (Wp.1 0M) first passing through an area of chestnut woodland, characteristic of this location.

Sweet Chestnut (Castanea sativa)

The Sweet Chestnut (Castanea sativa), a genus of Fagaceae, the Beech Family, is cultivated both for its appearance and for the economic value of the fruit and timber. Originating from Europe and West Asia, it has naturalized across the island and is particularly prevalent in the **Curral** valley.

.. the old road into Curral

Descending the path, the old road into **Curral** soon comes into view on the right (Wp.2 8M), where it is carved on a precarious ledge against the steep rock face and snakes down the mountainside passing through tunnels along its descent.

Continuing down the pathway, we take in wonderful views of **Pico Grande** (Wp.3 20M) with its unmistakable rocky stack at the summit before eventually reaching an exposed rock projection (Wp.4 35M), which offers good views down the valley and is a lovely place to stop for a rest.

Pico Grande

The natural flora along this route includes Carline Thistles, Madeira Mountain Stock, marigolds, geraniums and one or two rare orchids, as well as the huge Black Parsley and Sow Thistles, all of course depending on the time of year visited.

The final stretch of the walk runs alongside the cultivated terraces before beginning a short ascent through the woodland, which in early spring, is carpeted with lovely yellow Celandines.

Around 25 metres before reaching the road, another landslide had completely obliterated the final section of path which lead parallel with the road to reach a picnic table. At this point, red arrows on rocks divert the route down stone and concrete steps to reach the road and the end of the walk (Wp.5 75M). If you are making an immediate return to base from this point, the bus stop is approximately 300 metres up the road to the right (Wp.6).

Those wishing to visit the village should continue up the road for around half a kilometre to reach the centre where you can enjoy a drink or refreshments in one of the cafés or bars. Taxis are available beside the cafés; the cost back to **Eira da Serrada** will be around €10. Bus users will find the bus stop at the bottom of the main street at the start of the one-way system.

8 ECOLOGICAL PARK:
RIBEIRA DAS CALES - MONTE - BABOSAS
(PR3.1 CAMINHO REAL DO MONTE

The **Ecological Park** occupies an area of around 1000 hectares and is situated in the mountainous area above **Funchal**, extending at its most northerly point to **Pico Areeiro**. Created in 1994 with nature conservation as its prime objective, it offers environmental education and recreational facilities for residents and visitors.

This interesting route starts from the Reception Centre and descends two kilometers through the park before continuing on an ancient trail, an original footpath linking the north coast villages with **Funchal**. At around the halfway point the path emerges onto the regional road at **Terreiro da Luta** providing an opportunity to visit the statue of **Our Lady of Peace**, an historic monument erected in a superb elevated setting, giving fine views over **Funchal**.

Our final section descends the famous *Calvario* route, passing a number of the stations of the cross before arriving in **Largo do Fonte** from where we skirt around the historic centre passing tropical gardens, palaces, the church of **Nossa Senhora do Monte**, the toboggans and the cable car, before finally ending in **Babosas** square.

Make this into a memorable circular route by taking the bus from **Funchal** up to the park, then at the end of the walk, descend to the city on the *teleférico* (cable car).

Access by hire car or taxi: take the ER103 from **Funchal** passing through the centre of **Monte** parish and continuing in the direction of **Poiso**.

The Reception Centre and car park at **Ribeira das Cales** are located approximately 5 km north of **Monte** on the left of the road.

The Reception Centre at Ribeira des Cales

Access by bus: Funchal buses Nºs 56, 103 or 138 serve the **Ecological Park**. Return to **Funchal** from **Monte** on bus Nºs 20, 21, or 48 or from **Babosas** on bus Nº22.

In 2010 a series of fires raged over the central area of the island badly affecting the forests and mountains; the Ecological Park was on of the worst hit areas, with around 95% of its vegetation damaged. Nevertheless, nature heals quickly and the undergrowth and low vegetation is recovering well, unfortunately the forest will take much longer, but a dedicated programme of tree clearance and restoration is in place. Perhaps one positive is that we now have great views from the park and particularly from **Pico Alto.**

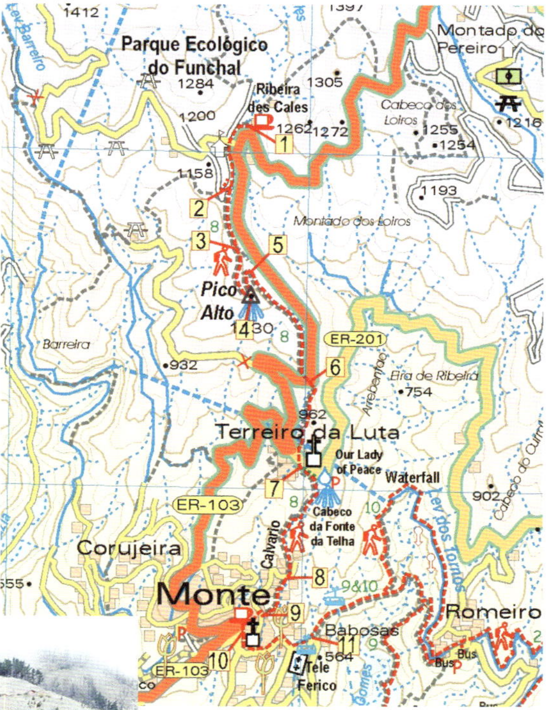

The amazing view from Pico Alto

The sign at the start

Our walk begins at a signpost at the rear of the reception centre (Wp.1 0M), which directs us down a flight of steps through a well-planted garden and over a bridge to meet a junction where we continue ahead. Soon crossing a tarred forest road, we pick up the path on the opposite side. At the next junction we reach a cobbled road again picking up the path on the opposite side (Wp.2 7M).

The trail descends towards a water tank; there's a 'field code' sign on a path to our right, which leads back to the cobbled road, but our route continues ahead passing the nursery where it becomes a little rocky underfoot.

We soon reach another path off to our right (Wp.3 18M), this is our route up the hillside to reach the end of the cobbled road at a large picnic and barbecue area. Going left from the road, we continue on a flight of paved steps ascending to a *miradouro* at **Pico Alto** (1129 metres) (Wp.4 27M).

Let's pause here to admire the fantastic view of Funchal (cloud permitting) and the surrounding forests and slopes, before leaving on the opposite side of the platform to take a narrow path left just before a group of rock boulders.

Descending from Pico Alto

The path leads us down the hillside on a gradual zigzag descent before straightening and levelling out where again we see the picnic area, now at a higher level than us. Here we keep an eye out for a stepped path turning sharply right (Wp.5 34M), descending this to reach a junction and turn right again. The path follows the contours of the hillside before the descent steepens with frequent flights of steps, before we reach the ER103 regional road (Wp.6 54M).

Leaving the park, we continue on the opposite side of the road picking up the ancient cobbled pathway, the fast flowing **Levada das Cales** running beside us. Descending quite steeply, we soon arrive at a junction with the ER103 and ER201 regional roads at **Terreiro da Luta** (Wp.7 69M).

Our Lady Of Peace

The path continues on the opposite side of the road, but we have an option here to leave our trail to visit the impressive monument of Our Lady of Peace; inaugurated in 1927, this five and half metre statue stands on columns looking south to the coast.

It's reputed that the rosary at the base of the statue was formed from fragments of chain from ships sunk in **Funchal** harbour during the First World War, these were transported manually during a pilgrimage to **Terreiro da Luta**. This landmark can be found 200 metres along the ER201.

Also of interest is the lovely **Quinta do Terreiro da Luta**. Originally built as a railway station, it was the highest point of the **Monte** railway which closed in 1914. The station building has been restored and there are enchanting gardens at the rear with fantastic views of **Funchal** bay as well as an impressive bronze statue of João Gonçalves Zarco, Madeira's most important historical figure and founder of the island. Unfortunately the *quinta* was closed to the public in 2014 though may reopen at some point in the future.

Back on our trail, we continue on the ancient **Caminho do Monte** path descending a leafy lane to pass the 14th to the 6th Stations of the Cross, which appear at intervals along the descent. After a few minutes we pass the **Spring of the Shepherdess** where in 1495 the Lady of Monte is said to have appeared.

After reaching the first houses we pick up a tarred road for a few metres before rejoining the path, signed 'Caminho das Lajinhas' (Wp.8 85M). From this point we leave the pilgrimage route as our path descends through an old area of **Monte**, passing between quaint rural houses and gardens as it twists and turns quite steeply before ending at a junction where two tarred roads meet. Crossing over, we pick up the trail again (Wp.9 100M) as we enter **Monte** gardens arriving at the 1st station of the cross on the path above the village square.

The route leads us around the church of **Senhora do Monte** and as we approach the front we turn right behind a row of church cottages leading us gently down into **Largo da Fonte** (Wp.10 105M).

The bustling square exudes the charm of bygone days, with the bandstand, cafés, monuments, shrines and souvenir stalls to interest us. Our final section takes us from the square along **Caminho das Babosas** passing **Monte Palace Tropical Gardens** on our right and the start of the toboggan run where white-clad *carreiros* with their wickerwork sledges, make a splendid spectacle.

The *carreiros* and their toboggans

Continuing along the cobbled road we arrive at the cable car station for our optional journey back into **Funchal**; the trail ends a little further along the cobbled road in **Babosas** square (Wp.11 120M).

9 MONTE - BOM SUCESSO - FUNCHAL

Please note that at the time of our update (Nov 18) this trail remained closed due to erosion of the pathways and *levada* following severe fire damage in 2016. Unlike most other water channels, this *levada* is privately owned and therefore repair work is not at the discretion of the authorities, but hopefully the trail will reopen some time in the future. Therefore please check with the Tourist Office or your hotel on the current status of this route, before setting out.

This trail explores the deep gorge between **Monte** and the **Botanical Gardens**, before leading us under the **Via Rápida** bridge to make a final descent to the sea front of **Funchal**.

Our Lady of Monte church

The path through the woods is very steep in places and care is needed with the steps. Along the route, we also follow **Levada do Bom Sucesso**, which has a few tricky and precipitous sections. Nevertheless, this is a superb walk, made circular by taking the *teleférico* from **Old Town** to **Monte** and also makes a memorable day out if we combine it with a visit to the historic centre of **Monte**.

* with *teleférico*

Access by car hire or taxi:
Follow the ER103 from Funchal to **Monte**. The main car park is situated just above the village.

The cable car station (the *teleférico*)

Access by bus:
Town Buses N°s 20, 21, 22 & 48 serve **Monte** and **Babosas**. Alternatively take the *teleférico* for a spectacular ascent from **Funchal** seafront.

Access by *teleférico*:
The **Funchal**/**Monte** *teleférico* is situated on the seafront in **Funchal Old Town**.

The route starts in **Babosas** square; situated just below the **Funchal** *teleférico* terminus (Wp.1 0M). Here we take the cobbled lane down into the valley, passing the cable car station for the **Botanical Gardens**, to arrive at a junction where the path to **Levada dos Tornos** turns off left to climb up the wooded valley. (Wp.2 12M). Our route continues down the cobbled path to the right, signed 'Levada do Bom Sucesso'. After crossing the pretty stone bridge over the **Ribeira de João Gomes** (Wp.3) we climb up to a path junction where **Curral dos Romeiros** is signed to the left and **Levada do Bom Sucesso** to the right (Wp.4 22M).

Descending to the Botanical Gardens

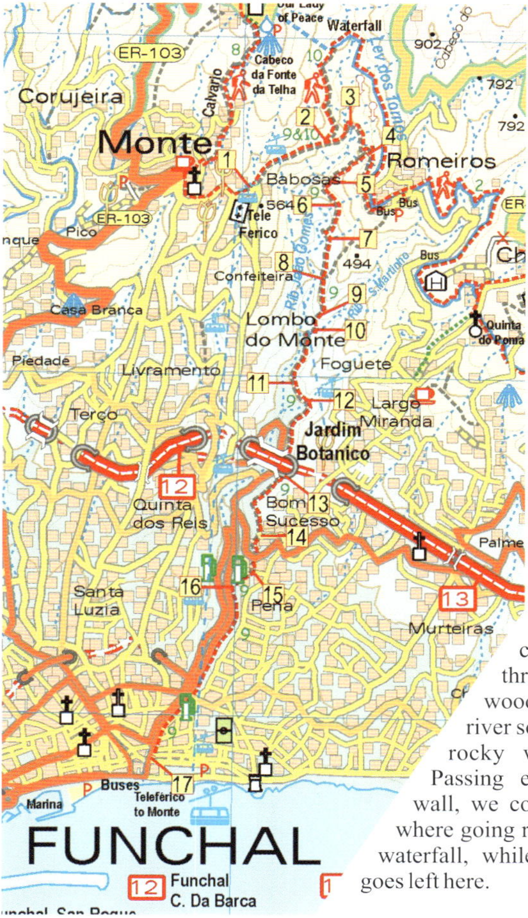

We turn right off the main track and drop down the eastern side of the valley on a log-stepped descent, with the remains of rustic handrails lining the woodland path in places. This is such an attractive route and looking across to our right we can see the *teleférico* on its spectacular route above the tree canopy.

A particularly steep zigzag (Wp.5 30M) brings us to a flat clearing before we continue down through the forest on wooden steps, churning river sounds rising from the rocky watercourse below. Passing evidence of an old wall, we come to a T-junction, where going right will take us to a waterfall, while our onward route goes left here.

Our path levels out for a section, passing a cave on the left (Wp.6) before descending again alongside the steep gorge with its rushing water. Another

Madeira Walks 1 49

steep descent (46M) brings us close to the river before we cross a rock-filled gully (Wp.7) to contour along the valley wall in gentle descents. The impressive **Via Rápida** bridge, now dominates the view ahead.

.. large Agaves adorn our route ..

A red and yellow waymark (Wp.8) confirms our route just before a junction with a path climbing up to our left; this leads to **Curral dos Romeiros**, though the signpost no longer exists. We come across a small area where large Agaves adorn our route, perhaps escapes from the **Botanical Gardens**.

At the next faint path junction at the bottom of a flight of steps (Wp.9) we keep right, to descend beside flimsy guard rails before passing log steps which climb up to the left and then stone steps. A wire guard rail bring us down to a stone bridge (Wp.10 68M) at the start of the **Levada do Bom Sucesso**, marking the end of the woodland descent.

Following it, we edge round a rock face to walk above sheer drops before reaching a less vertiginous section (Wp.11) facing the **Via Rápida** bridge. We curve into a small side valley beneath the remains of a substantial house, then cross an aqueduct bridge on stepping stones between rocks, which needs very careful footwork as some of the slabs are missing (Wp.12).

Coming out of the valley, we are hit by traffic noise as we stroll along to pass under the **Via Rápida** (Wp.13 87M), our path running below the *levada* for a short section before coming back onto its wall; the houses of **Bom Sucesso** now come into view.

The tricky section at Wp.12

As we pass the first house, we come to the end of the tarmaced **Rua Antonio Costa Medico** (Wp.14), to take a pedestrian stairway down to our right. Descending between tight-packed houses, we reach a tarmac road (Wp.15 102M); crossing carefully, we go onto the **João Gomez** walkway to continue dropping down through the houses, passing walkways off to our left. More walkways branch off the main route as we continue steeply down to emerge from the **Travessa de Ribeira João Gomes** onto the pavement by the main road (Wp.16 107M).

Turning downhill, we stroll down pavements and across a tiny square, the road becoming fully commercialized, before we reach our finish at the taxi rank (Wp.17 121M) just before the sea front in **Funchal**.

10 LEVADA DOS TORNOS - MONTE - CURRAL ROMEIROS CIRCULAR

In bygone days, **Monte** was an area preferred by English settlers due to its peaceful location and cooler climate evidenced now by the legacy of colonial *quintas* and English gardens.

Monte palace gardens

Offering lots of variety, this circular trail from **Monte** to **Romeiros** starts in **Largo da Fonte**, passing beside palaces and gardens before ascending though lovely woodland with rocky crags, impressive waterfalls and spectacular deep valleys along the way.

Due to both its links with the past and its close proximity to **Funchal**, this atmospheric trail is extremely popular, particularly with English tourists, but it does come at a price; some sections are unprotected, running alongside deep drops where the railings are damaged or in some places non-existent. If in doubt, turn back at the waterfall and follow the route in reverse to **Romeiros**.

Access by hire car or taxi: follow the ER 103 from **Funchal** to **Monte**. The main car park is situated just above the village.

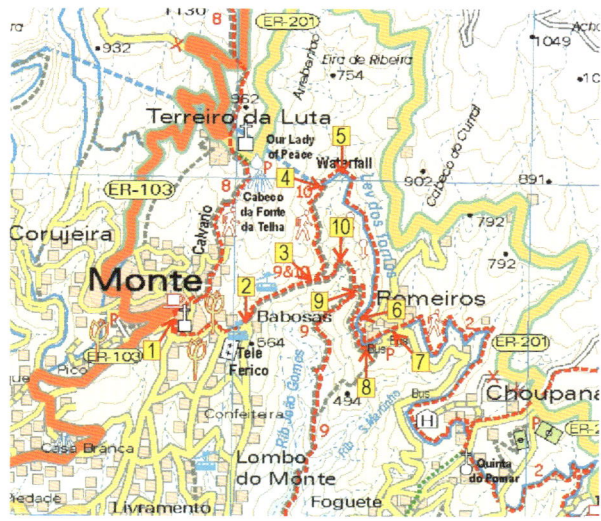

Access by public transport: Town Buses N°s 20, 21 & 48 serve **Monte** as does the *teleférico* (cable car) from **Funchal** seafront

Starting out from **Largo da Fonte** square, **Monte**'s main square (Wp.1 0M) we head along **Caminho das Babosas** curving round beside the **Monte Palace Tropical Gardens** - there's the option of a visit to these beautiful gardens before we head off on the trail, or alternatively on return. Continuing along the cobbled lane, we pass the **Church of Senhora do Monte**, the toboggan run and the **Funchal/Monte** *teleférico* before arriving in **Babosas** square (Wp.2 7M).

The cobbled lane continues, descending steeply into the valley, soon passing the **Jardim Botánico** *teleférico*, before reaching a path junction (Wp.3 15M) where the path to **Levada dos Tornos** turns off left. Also note that our return route emerges at this point following the ascent up the **Ribeira de João Gomes** valley (Wp.3 90M).

The Levada dos Tornos tunnel

Our outward trail runs along the valley wall, swinging left (17M) on an energetic uphill climb, getting steeper between the cliffs and the plunging valley before our final ascent to meet the **Levada dos Tornos** (Wp.4 31M) where it emerges from a tunnel. At around 1500 metres long, the tunnel starts in the southern area of the **Ecological Park**, the channel passing below **Terreiro da Luta** on its course east.

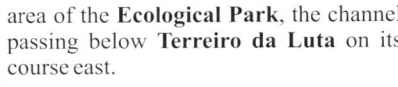

Ignoring this, we follow the *levada* downstream, immediately arriving at an impressive waterfall, where **Ribeira das Cales** plunges into the riverbed below (Wp.5 35M).

We pass beneath the waterfall through a short tunnel; care is needed as we emerge to different scenery; the wooded slopes are replaced by sheer cliffs as we negotiate the eastern side of the **Ribeira de João Gomes** valley.

.. an impressive waterfall ..

Passing another waterfall, careful footwork is again needed along the next section until we reach a sluice gate on the channel (40M). From this position we have good views down to **Funchal** harbour.

Ignoring a path leading off to the right, a shortcut down into the valley (Wp.6),

Approaching Romeiros

our route becomes less exposed due to increased undergrowth.

The channel becomes covered over with slabs and a few minutes later we arrive in **Romeiros** village where we are directed from the channel, turning right down steps. The *levada* is signed here in both directions (Wp.7 60M).

Turning right at the bottom of the steps, we follow the road down to the bus stop and as the houses end, we turn right onto a traditional cobbled path in immaculate condition (Wp.8 65M). Contouring along we now have views over the steep **João Gomez** valley to **Babosas**.

Descending the eastern valley side amongst mimosa and eucalyptus on a steep zigzagged and stone-rippled section, we arrive at a junction with a path dropping down left (Wp.9 75M), the route to **Bom Sucesso** (Walk 9) below the **Botanical Gardens**.

Our trail continues ahead, the gradient moderating before leading us over an impressive stone bridge (Wp.10 80M). From the tumbling waters of the **Ribeira João Gomes** we make an ascent up the western forested slopes, to emerge from the trees at the junction with our outward path to **Levada dos Tornos** (Wp.3 90M).

Still climbing, we again pass the **Botánico Teleférico**, before a final steep ascent brings us up to **Babosas** square. Another five minutes walking and we are back in **Largo da Fonte** for a well-earned rest and refreshments (Wp.1 110M).

11 LEVADA DA AZENHA - (PR23 CAMINHO VELHO DO CASTELO)

'Short and Sweet' is perhaps the best description for this new PR trail close to the town of **Caniço**. It's a quaint and scenic route, but perhaps best suited to those staying along the south east of the island; it's not really worth the effort of a long drive unless linked with another walk or activity. That said, it is a very enjoyable trail and we decided to include it, not only as one of the official walking trails, but because it really is quite charming and interesting and provides an opportunity to observe and imagine the past cultures of the area.

Access by car or taxi:
Leave the VR1 at Junction 16 turning right at the next junction to follow the new bypass signed 'Caniço & Camacha'. After 1 km, go right at a roundabout taking the first left beside 'The Pub'. At the top of this short road, go left along the ER204 for 500 metres taking a right turn signed 'Azinha'. Parking is available on the narrow lane to the left of the junction. The *levada* is signed 60 metres down the ER204 on the left hand side.

Access by bus:
There's a frequent service on numerous Horários and SAM buses running along the ER204 to and from **Funchal** passing through **Caniço**, **Assomada** and **Santa Cruz**. Alight at **Sitio da Azenha** bus stop. The *levada* is signed on the road 100 m below the row of shops.

A *levada*-side cottage

Starting in **Sitio da Azenh**a, there's a finger post and information panel at the side of a house on the ER204 (Wp.1 0M). We turn left to follow the narrow channel upstream where it initially runs parallel with the road.

Views to Caniço church

One hundred metres along we pass beside a pretty cottage then older houses and gardens before the route bears left. We're now at a quite high level where each property has its own stairway down to the road. Looking back, there's a good view of **Caniço** church giving some perspective to how close the channel is to the town. Veering left again, we pass alongside a rock wall, the valley to our right is deepening but there are steel posts and wire to protect us.

.. a new stone bridge ..

We cross a new stone bridge over a river to reach the old water mill (Wp.2 8M), the water once feeding the mill shooting down beside it. The mill itself is in a bad condition and sadly only its walls and three grinders remain. Turning right in front of the building we climb log steps up the hillside, where we pick up the *levada* again from where it flows high above the mill to reach the chute. Substantial rustic fencing has been erected on the stairway protecting us from the deep gorge to our right. Going left again, we head off into another valley, this one lined with acacia mimosa and lots of giant reeds which provide us with protection against the drop to our right.

Arriving at another new section of fencing, we find a charming wooden bridge across the gorge (Wp.3 20M). At this point we leave the *levada* and it's now straight ahead of us, coming down the hillside. As we descend to the bridge, there are two fingerposts; one directs us over the bridge, signed 'Caminho Velha do Castelo 0.3km'; the other points back on our trodden path signed 'Levada da Azenha 1 km'.

Over the bridge, we enjoy the tranquility with only the sound of the birds, as we climb a short rocky hillside with masses of wild flora. There are Bermuda buttercups, Mauritius nightshade, brambles and prickly pears as well as carpets of Nasturtiums; it's so quiet and picturesque that it's difficult to believe we're so close to the town.

Houses appear above us and reaching a junction with a narrow *levada*, we step over turning left onto a concrete drive then going right between houses, one with a garden stocked with Bird of Paradise (Strelitzia reginae), Madeira's national flower; there are good views of **Caniçal** from this elevated position. Winding between the houses for a short distance, our trail comes to an abrupt end as we reach a lane beside new houses (Wp.4 30M). We have to admit that we felt a stab of disappointment at this point; it's such a short route and we didn't want it to end so quickly, but the return route is just as enjoyable and gives us different perspectives all the way back to our starting point in **Sitio da Azenha** (Wp.1 60M).

Back on the ER204, it's approximately 300 metres uphill to reach **Snack Bar Azenha**, making a pleasant end to our 'short and sweet' walk.

12 SÃO LOURENÇO - PRAINHA - PICO DA PIEDADE

Breathtaking scenery, wild landscapes, amazing rock formations - **São Lourenço** is unique. Unlike most of the island, it's quite arid, providing a habitat for a number of rare endemic plants. Around the peninsula, dragon trees (Dracaena draco), once native to the area, have also been planted alongside exotic Agava attenuata and red sword aloe.

This trail, an alternative to the well-known route across the peninsula may be short, but it's equally stunning and offers a number of options for a memorable day out.

Climbing firstly to the ancient chapel on **Pico da Piedade**, the route then drops down to the **Prainha**, the island's only natural sandy beach, for a few hours swimming or sunbathing. There's also a beach bar open throughout the summer period and at weekends.

Pico da Piedade

Close by is **Quinta do Lorde**, the impressive holiday resort recently created around the **Caniçal** marina. Its popular **Captain's Bar** is open daily.

* summer and weekends

Access by car or taxi:
Take the VR1 to the **Caniçal** roundabout following the signs for **Prainha** and **São Lourenço**. Roadside parking is available at **Prainha**.

Access by bus:
SAM Bus N°113 provides a frequent daily service from **Funchal** to the peninsula via **Machico** and **Caniçal**.

We start the walk a few metres east of the **Prainha** lay-by (Wp.1 0M) where a gate abuts a paved driveway leading down into the valley below. After a sharp U-bend the driveway continues down to the beach, but just beyond the bend we take a narrow path off left (Wp.2 5M) and a few metres ahead, after passing the first dragon tree, turn right,

56 Madeira Walks 1

climbing slightly to reach six old stone bollards. Fifteen metres ahead, a narrow path drops down on our right - we return to this point for our final descent to the beach, but for now we continue ahead for a few metres to reach a broad earthen track.

Quinta do Lorde and the marina

Our route turns right, following the track for a short distance to reach a cobbled stairway on the right (Wp.3 15M), our route to the chapel. As we climb, both north and south coastlines come into view, the eastern lowlands stretch out around us and **Quinta do Lorde** and the marina are down to our left.

The steps make an easy zigzag up the hillside, soon arriving on the summit beside the **Capela Nossa Senhora de Piedade** (Wp.4 20M), location for the annual festival of Our Lady of Mercy (Nossa Senhora da Piedade), patron saint of fishermen.

Each year on the third weekend of September, a procession leaves **Caniçal** in a flotilla of decorated boats on its route to **Quinta do Lorde**, the pilgrimage then continuing on foot up to the chapel.

Capela Nossa Senhorsa de Piedade

Leaving this stunning viewpoint, we retrace our steps down to the track and head back towards the stone bollards, but now around fifteen metres before reaching the bollards, our route turns off left towards the beach (Wp.5).

Crossing over the grassy hillside heading towards the beach, the narrow path becomes a little vague in places but soon arrives in front of a large rock below the cliffs. Going right and descending towards the dragon trees and red aloes, the trail emerges onto a wide path and gully.

Around the next bend the gully turns off left (Wp.6), our route continuing along the line of exotic aloes before rejoining the paved driveway to reach the beach bar (Wp.7 40M).
Steps lead down to the sandy cove hemmed in by the large sea cliffs; it's idyllic, particularly during the quieter winter season. After a swim or a spell of sunbathing it's time to tear ourselves away and head back. Now ignoring the paved track, we take the left hand concrete drive behind the bar to reach steps ascending on the left.

Red sword aloes on the approach to the beach

This paved stairway zigzags steadily up the hillside leading us back to the starting point (Wp.8 55M), though while in the area, it's well worth visiting **Quinta do Lorde**. The road into the village can be found 500 metres east of the **Praia** car park.

Resort Quinta do Lorde

Set in a beautiful bay beside the marina, this new coastal village has been built in an architectural style sympathetic with the area and its surroundings.

Spreading up from the coastline and marina, the complex is hemmed in by the surrounding cliffs and hillside and comprises a hotel, houses, apartments, restaurants, swimming areas, leisure facilities, a market and a church

Quinta do Lorde

13 ARCO DE SÃO JORGE TO BOA VENTURA

Arco de São Jorge, the most westerly parish of **Santana**, and **Boa Ventura**, a parish of **São Vicente**, lie in a lush forested area of the north coast, the latter nestling at the northern edge of the **Ribeira Porco** valley, spreading down from the central mountain range. **Boa Ventura** is a small agricultural village clustered around the church, which stands on a cobbled terrace overlooking the village and the mountains.

The ER101 connects these two small communities, twisting and climbing for 5.5 kilometres and passing through two tunnels en-route. Prior to their construction in the 1950s, access between these two communities was only possible along the **Caminho da Entrosa** path, which is cut into the sea cliffs. This is the route we follow on this stunning walk, which rewards us with superb views along the coastline, wonderful natural vegetation and interesting rock formations.

This walk can be approached either from **Arco de São Jorge** or in the opposite direction from **Boa Ventura** so could be done there-and-back or one way (as per the symbols below), using taxi or bus to link start and finishing points.

Access by hire car or taxi: from the west, approach via **Ribeira Brava** and **São Vicente** taking the VE1 east to **Boa Ventura**, then follow the ER101 to the starting point at **Arco de São Jorge** (14.5 km). From the east, approach via **Santana** on the VE1 continuing west on the ER101 to **Arco de São Jorge**.

The walk

starts at **Restaurante O Arco** situated on the coastal side of the road, west of the village and ends in **Boa Ventura**. A taxi back to our start point costs around €15.

Access by bus: Rodoeste Bus N°6 **Funchal - Boaventura** and **Arco de São Jorge**, via **São Vicente**. Horário Bus N°s 103 & 138 leave **Boa Ventura**, passing through **Arco de São Jorge** and **Santana** on the return to Funchal.

The old trail begins at **Restaurante O Arco** (Wp.1 0M) following a cobbled path which initially runs alongside agricultural plots and small garden orchards, lined a little further along with Australian Cheesewood; an introduced species which produces fragrant flowers in spring and large orange berries in autumn. Although this fast growing and attractive tree provides dense shade for the agricultural crops, it is one of Madeira's invasive plants, threatening areas of natural vegetation.

Indigenous flora soon takes over as our route begins a short climb to a fine viewpoint high above the sea cliffs (Wp.2 10M); it's possible to see along the coast to **Porto Moniz**, while lying directly below is **São Cristovão** and **Boa Ventura**, our destination. The pathway to this point is quite wide though erosion was found on one section during our latest survey (2013), so care is needed.

Ilhéu Preto and Ilhéu Vermelho

From this panoramic vantage point we take in the expanse of the ocean, gloriously turquoise and crystal clear with white surf breaking on the tiny islets of **Ilhéu Preto** and **Ilhéu Vermelho** just out from the coast.

At this point the path starts its steep descent, zigzagging down the almost vertical cliff; in parts, carved into the rock face. The path is still quite wide, though we found damage due to landslips on two sections, so care is needed while negotiating this descent. On the approach to sea level our trail meets another path (Wp.3 30M) in front of an old stone barn. Going right here leads to the headland and the ruins of an old sugar cane mill (Wp.4 35M).

Madeira Sea Stock

Much of the vegetation along the route is typical of other coastal areas, but there are a number of exceptions; during spring and summer many endemic species are found in flower including White Everlasting, Stonecrops, Golden Musschia, Madeira Germander, Madeira Sea Stock, Carline Thistles and chrysanthemums.

No one will fail to spot the magnificent specimens of Houseleek which thrive here; the disc Houseleek or Saucer plant (Aeonium glandulosum) clings to the rock face while the Viscid Houseleek (Aeonium glutinosum) appears everywhere along the route.

Disc Houseleek

After taking that short detour and returning to the junction, our **Caminho da Entrosa** path continues in front of the old barn descending down to a stone bridge (Wp.5 43M), which we cross before climbing up to **São Cristovão**. Just before the bridge, there is another path to the right which makes a short detour beside red clay walls to more ruins at the mouth of the river, an option for anyone wanting to leave the main trail to extend the walk.

Our route continues from the bridge and climbs around 65 metres to **São Cristovão**, soon passing through denser vegetation. Towards the top, a path alongside a narrow *levada* (Wp.6 57M) leads us to **Bar Restaurante São Cristovão** (Wp.7 60M) from where we have wonderful views of the coastline and of the whole of the **Entrosa** trail as it zigzags steeply down the cliffs. To the south lie the forested slopes of the central mountain range with the full expanse of the **Ribeira Porco** valley, also in view.

.. the view east from the bar-restaurante ..

From the restaurant it's a 1.7 kilometre walk on a tarred road, climbing past agricultural buildings and new property to arrive beside an electricity tower on the regional road, close to the village centre of **Boa Ventura** (Wp.8 100M). The bus stop is directly opposite the tower.

14 SANTANA - FAJÃ DA ROCHA DO NAVIO

One of **Santana**'s best kept secrets, our trail leads to an ancient coastal settlement with a distinctive feel of bygone days. It's quiet, remote and until fairly recently was only accessible by an old path carved into the rock descending 365 metres to sea level. Once there, you can walk along the *fajã* and across the pebbly beach to the small islet of **Ilhéu da Rocha do Navio**, situated a few metres from the shore which becomes cut off at high tide. Fertile agricultural plots continue to be tended, access now made easier by the construction of a cable car (*teleférico*) operating at specific times during the week.

Grapes, the dominant crop, are harvested at the beginning of September. Small agricultural barns and shelters are scattered here and a few weekend retreats; the largest building is the nature reserve and education centre, its gardens devoted to the growth of endemic flora.

A weekend retreat

In 2001 **Rocha do Navio Nature Reserve** became part of the Nature 2000 Network as a site of community interest and is now protected by Parque Natural da Madeira. Of particular interest is the potential habitat of Mediterranean monk seals, dolphins and marine and terrestrial birds as well as rare endemic plant species found on the islets.

Our trail begins at **Santana** church, first dropping down a country lane to reach the *teleférico* station, then descending on ancient pathway and steps. The gradient is quite steep in places and some sections have been eroded, so care is needed, but there are no precipitous drops and protective fencing is in place where necessary. We return by *teleférico*, making this a great circular route.

* with *teleférico*   ** in Santana centre

Access by car or taxi:
From the south and east follow the VE1 to the **Santana** roundabout, turning left into the centre of the town. There is a car park on the right, across from the civic centre and the A-framed houses and gardens. The walk starts from the church situated close by in the town centre.

Access by bus:
There is a regular bus service (N°s 56, 103 & 138) from **Funchal** to **Santana** centre. The walk starts beside the church.

Starting on the left of the church (Wp.1 0M), we follow **Rua da Igreja**, a narrow rural lane heading in the direction of the coast. As we leave the houses behind we reach a junction with another lane on the right, signed 'Rocha da Navio Teleférico' (Wp.2 15M) which we take.

The *teleférico*

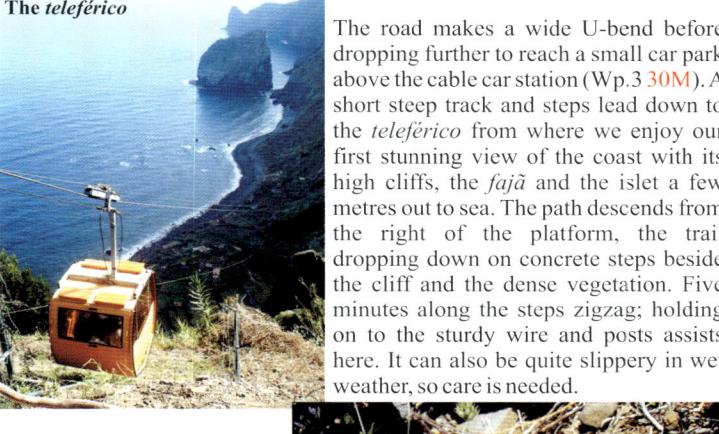

The road makes a wide U-bend before dropping further to reach a small car park above the cable car station (Wp.3 30M). A short steep track and steps lead down to the *teleférico* from where we enjoy our first stunning view of the coast with its high cliffs, the *fajã* and the islet a few metres out to sea. The path descends from the right of the platform, the trail dropping down on concrete steps beside the cliff and the dense vegetation. Five minutes along the steps zigzag; holding on to the sturdy wire and posts assists here. It can also be quite slippery in wet weather, so care is needed.

.. steep steps ..

Prickly pear

Prickly pear, globularia and throatwort thrive here; at about eight minutes the path levels as it rounds a valley head, the deep gorge to our left dropping down to the sea.

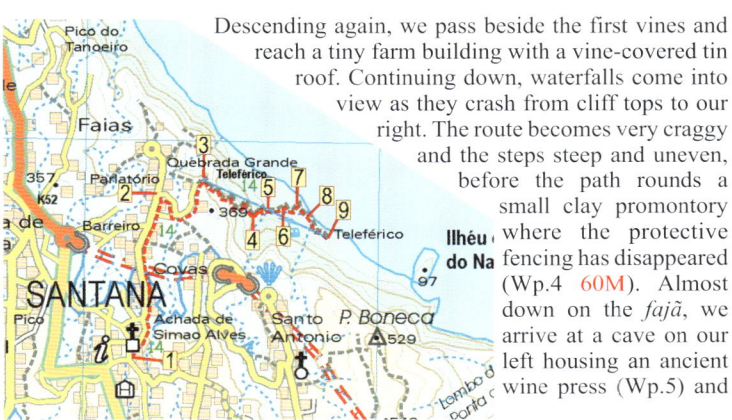

Descending again, we pass beside the first vines and reach a tiny farm building with a vine-covered tin roof. Continuing down, waterfalls come into view as they crash from cliff tops to our right. The route becomes very craggy and the steps steep and uneven, before the path rounds a small clay promontory where the protective fencing has disappeared (Wp.4 60M). Almost down on the *fajã*, we arrive at a cave on our left housing an ancient wine press (Wp.5) and just below, we cross over a narrow *levada* with a branch heading down beside our path. On reaching the first house and storage barns (Wp.6 70M), our route turns right passing vineyards and a well on our right. Spring brings a colourful floral carpet of nasturtiums, sea stocks, marigolds and thistles.

We reach another junction; our route will go straight ahead, but first we go left to drop down to the Nature Reserve (Wp.7 75M), open only at specific times and usually by arrangement, though the small grounds are accessible, planted with endemic coastal plants including dragon trees, Echium nervosum, Mandon's chrysanthemum, butcher's broom and houseleeks. Returning to the junction, our path turns left, passing one or two small properties before we cross over a stream on a pretty hump-backed bridge (Wp.8 85M). The pebbly shore is now to our left and pretty passageways and gateways to cottages and barns, appear on our right.

There are always one or two farmers or fishermen around ready to have a friendly chat; otherwise, it's quiet and peaceful and when the sun is shining and the sea is blue, it's paradise. At the end of the cultivated area we reach the cable car (Wp.9 90M) and from here take a five minute spectacular journey back to the station, fromwhere we retrace our steps to the starting point in **Santana** (Wp.1 120M).

.. storage barns ..

The Nature Reserve

.. passing passageways ..

Operating times for the Cable Car:
Saturday & Sunday
From 9.00am - 10.00am, 12.00 noon - 1.00pm, 6.00pm - 7.00pm
Wednesday
From 9.00am - 10.00am, 12.00 noon - 12.30pm, 6.00 pm - 7.00pm
Fridays
From 6.00pm - 7.00pm only

15 LEVADA DO CANIÇAL (EAST)

Few people realise that the **Levada do Caniçal** continues beyond the road tunnel; whilst the start beneath a quarry is unimpressive, the main part of our route passes through beautiful countryside and woodland which has escaped the depredations of the area's expansion and new highway.

Caniçal, a parish of **Machico** situated 20 kilometres north-east of **Funchal**, is now an important area accommodating the island's new industrial port: agriculture and fishing being originally its main industry. Our trail, along a vast escarpment, circles the northern boundary of the town and en-route provides stunning views of the coastline to the **São Lourenço** peninsula with the **Desertas** islands also in view to the south.

Access by hire car or taxi: from **Machico**, follow the ER109 regional road towards **Caniçal**. The walk begins on the eastern side of **Túnel do Caniçal** where parking is available in a lay-by alongside a quarry and maintenance depot, a few metres from the tunnel entrance.

Access by bus: SAM bus N°113 provides a frequent service between **Funchal** and the **São Lourenço Peninsula** passing through **Machico** and **Caniçal**. Alight at the eastern side of **Túnel do Caniçal**.

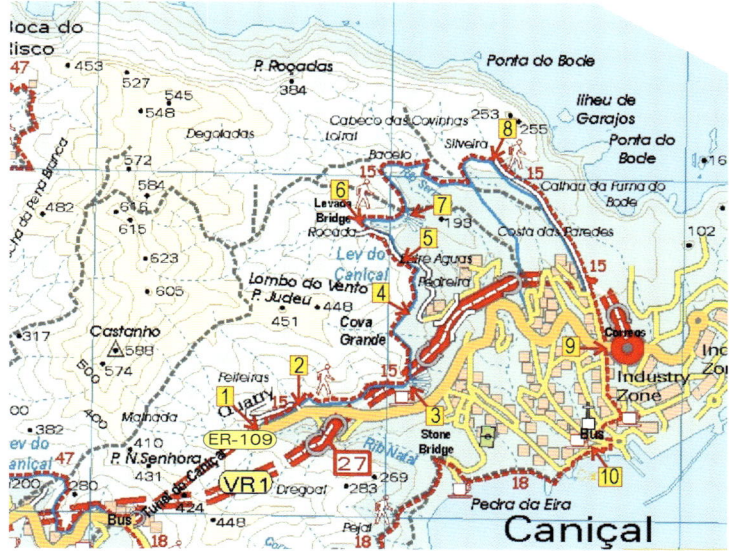

Stairs at the western end of the road tunnel lead up to a shrine, worthy of a quick peep, whilst at the bottom of the steps (Wp.1 0M), the **Levada do Caniçal** leaves the road on the left to traverse a handrail section. We can either follow the channel from this point, or pick up the *levada* at the top of the quarry access road (Wp.2 5M), thus avoiding the first short section, signed 'danger of falling rocks'. From the quarry, the *levada* has been reinstated along its whole length with safety fencing added where necessary, a noticeable change since our last edition.

The trail runs alongside a boulder wall and beside a cliff face before passing below a craggy escarpment where we take in our first views of the coastline. Rounding a bluff (Wp.3 17M), we head north across grassy slopes into the **Cova Grande** valley.

On approaching the uppermost houses of **Caniçal** we have fine views over the **São Lourenço** peninsula from this elevated position; here we lingered on a rocky spot beneath a solitary Cypress tree (Wp.4 26M) to take in the views and to watch the spectacular aerobatics of a male Kestrel lower down the escarpment.

The hillside becomes steeper and wilder as we curve into another valley; ahead are huts and cultivated terraces served by a dirt road that climbs up the valley and replaces the *levada* path (Wp.5 30M).

The views from Wp.4

Below a large hut, we leave the dirt road on the right, to follow the water channel as it swings left into a tree-filled valley and as we stroll through the acacia woodland we reach a new bridge over the valley's watercourse (Wp.6 37M).

From the bridge, we walk through the flower-filled woodland to come out of the trees to views over the peninsula (Wp.7 41M), our route now curving through more open woodland into another valley. Across the valley floor, the *levada* heads out to pass the remains of huts and terraces before crossing a water runoff bridged over the watercourse.

We swing into another tree-filled valley, now with eucalyptus appearing, the water channel edged with a riot of flowers enhanced by the frequent appearance of Red Admiral and Monarch butterflies.

Red Admiral

Crossing a watercourse and an earthen track, the valley changes to open woodland before we reach a sandy track where the *levada* makes a 90° turn to the right (Wp.8 62M). We follow the fast flowing channel through the woodland for around 50 metres before climbing onto the wide earthen track to our left.

Our final stage is an easy stroll down the wide track where we enjoy spectacular views of the north side of the peninsula and of the impressive red dry creeks lying below the forested slopes to the west.

.. spectacular views of the north side of the peninsula ..

The track becomes a wide tarred road; the new **Cemiterio de Caniçal** building is now on the right. The road heads down towards the new port; to our left are wind turbines and solar panels. Approaching the bottom, avenues of new housing appear to our right before we reach a junction beside the *Correios* (post office) (Wp.9 80M) with the 'end of motorway' roundabout along the road on our left.

Across the junction, we follow **Estrada da Banda d'Além** down towards the new church before the street swings right to come into the centre of **Caniçal**. There are a number of bars and restaurants on this street as we approach a new road junction.

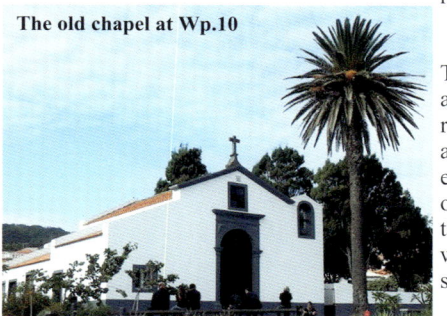

The old chapel at Wp.10

The bus stops and a taxi stand are on our right alongside the road but first we walk straight ahead into the lovely square to end our walk beside the pretty old chapel (Wp.10 84M). A taxi back to **Túnel do Caniçal** will cost €10. Bus users should return on bus Nº113.

16 LEVADA DO CASTELEJO - SÃO ROQUE

The **Ribeira de São Roque** valley rises from the foot of **Penha d'Águia** and extends to the forested slopes below **Ribeiro Frio**, with **Pico das Torres** and **Pico Ruivo** dominating the western vistas. **Levada do Castelejo** leads us through this mountainous landscape, adorned with lush vegetation, before transcending into the *laurisilva*, eventually bringing us to the source of *levada* in the **São Roque** riverbed.

It's a relatively easy walk along a comfortable path. The route is mainly protected with steel posts and wire fencing, except for some short sections around the water run-offs at valley heads and whilst the path underfoot is quite wide, care is needed on these sections.

Rock Navelwort
(*Umbilicus rupestris*)

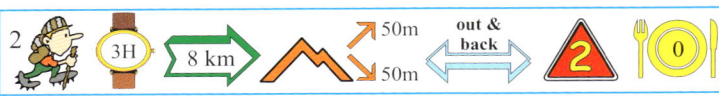

Leaving Cruz village

Access by car: follow the narrow road from the centre of **Cruz** village, signed 'Levada do Castelejo'. Keeping right at a junction, the *levada* crosses over the road just before the tarmac ends; there's adequate roadside parking above or below the channel.

Access by bus: bus route Nºs 53 and 78 serve **Cruz** village.

The hamlet of **Cruz**, lying on a mountain ridge between **Porto da Cruz** and **Faial**, is the starting point for this lovely walk. Heading westwards from the road junction (Wp.1 0M) we pass beside a few properties alongside agricultural terraces and vineyards our trail then sweeping left winding its way into the **São Roque** valley.

At this point we look across at the picturesque village of **São**

We head into the São Roque valley

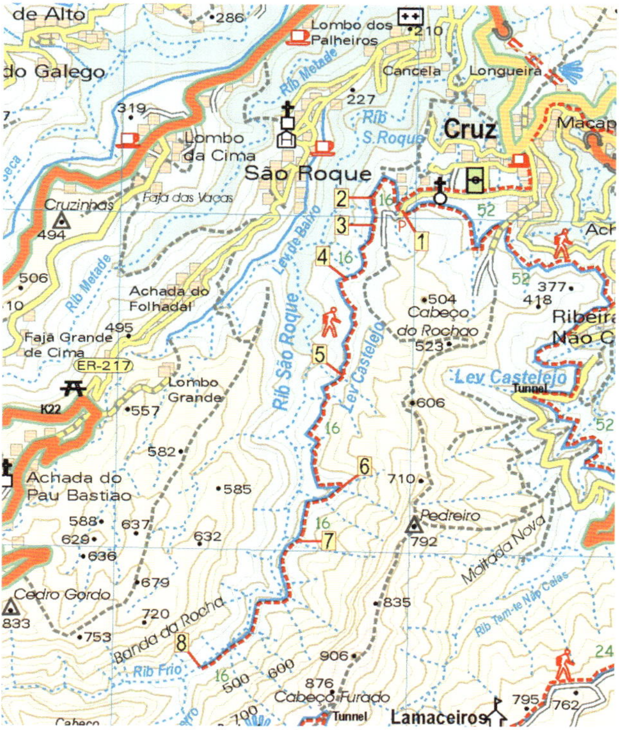

Roque do Faial, set against a backdrop of mountains with **Penha d'Águia** (**Eagle Rock**) and the north coast to our right.

Along this first section agricultural plots sweep down below us, the *levada* shoulder maintaining height as it follows the contours of the valley side (Wp.2 10M), where protective fencing starts.

Transcending into the forest

Along the opposite side of the valley, **Levada de Baixo** is clearly visible as is the high waterfall of **Água d'Alto** crashing over the valley side into the **São Roque River** (Wp.3 16M).

Leaving the plantations behind, we wind our way alongside rocky walls before the channel swings left again passing beneath overhanging rock (Wp.4 24M).

With stunning views all the way, we transcend into the natural forest where carpets of flowers adorn our route; White Eupatorium, Greater Periwinkle, Three-Cornered Leek and Red Flowering Sorrel are some of the species seen.

Madeira Walks 1   69

On reaching a valley head (Wp5 38M), a stream trickles over the *levada* before dropping into the valley below, an ideal habitat for a rich variety of ferns, mosses and lichens. We head into a deep gorge crossing a water run-off where the *levada* diverts into a stream (Wp.6 54M) soon crossing more valley heads. Approaching the main valley with the mountains and forested slopes above us, the **São Roque** riverbed becomes visible in the valley bottom (Wp.7 69M).

Fifteen minutes later we arrive at the source of the irrigation channel where the shoulder ceases, the *levada* now emerging from a tunnel through the rock face.

Steps to our right lead us down to the riverbed; sadly once a beautiful spot for a picnic, it's now a mass of rocks and boulders due to severe flooding in 2013; the main river now appears to have been diverted as part of the water management programme in the **Porto Cruz** area (Wp.8 85M).

Nevertheless, the mountain vistas compensate and there's another plus; a small picnic/barbecue area has been established on the opposite banking at the start of a newly recuperated trail into the woodland.

Views over São Roque and Faial

This new route has been amalgamated with this current walk and included in the list of official walking trails on Madeira. The new route will become **PR24 Vereda do Pico do Cedro Gordo & Levada do Casteleja** starting from **Cruz** village and ending in **São Roque de Faial** village. However at the time of our update (Nov 18), the route had not been included on the official tourism website.

17 PICO DO FACHO - MACHICO

The view from Pico do Facho

The first place on the island to be colonized and Madeira's capital during the first century of occupation, **Machico** is built around a lovely natural bay and, although relatively small, it now has a new marina and an attractive waterfront with sandy beaches, as well as a bustling centre with shops, bars and restaurants.

The Parochial Church of **Machico**, dedicated to Nossa Senhora da Conceição, is found in the main square framed by huge plane trees; it's well worth a visit. Our trail however, starts at the **Caniçal** tunnel leading us first to **Pico do Facho** (323 metres), which not only offers superb views over Madeira's east coast, the **São Lourenço** peninsula and the **Ilhas Desertas** but also provides a fantastic vantage point over **Funchal** airport; the aircraft seem close enough to pluck out of the sky as they make their landing approach to the runway. The final section of the route leads us down a donkey trail to end in the centre of the town.

Access by hire car or taxi: from **Machico**, follow the ER109 regional road towards **Caniçal**, parking at the entrance to **Túnel do Caniçal**.

Access by bus: take the Nº113 Machico-Caniçal bus.

From the entrance to the **Túnel do Caniçal** (Wp.1 0M), we set off up the **Pico do Facho** road. It's an energetic, steady ascent, rewarded by increasing panoramas over the **Machico** valley as we climb past the green gates of a water treatment site to the right, and a little further along and to our left, a cottage with its own fire engine.

We soon reach the point where the old **Machico-Caniçal** donkey trail crosses the road (Wp.2 18M), some fifteen metres before an electricity pylon, then continue to slog up the last few metres of the tarmac road, with views now opening up over **Caniçal** (Wp.3), before we turn right and come up to the parking area below **Pico do Facho**. Pathways take us up the slopes below the transmitter to find a suitable vantage point (Wp.4 23M).

Descending to the donkey trail at Wp.2

When we are sated with the views, we head back down the road - far easier down than up, of course - until we again reach the donkey trail (Wp.2 30M).

Turning left, we start to drop down the rough boulder path, often hidden by long grass, to come alongside a stone wall.

Our path divides (Wp.5 38M) and we go right and down across the sloping meadow, the path now more stone than grass. Coming below a small rock outcrop (Wp.6 50M), we go left. Our route, at times a narrow river of rubble, angles down across the meadow, and then curves right to drop towards a residential home which has cut the old trail, where we have to go left alongside the fencing to drop down onto a road (Wp.7 56M).

Once in front of the impressive building Casa da Misericórdia e Grace, roughly translating to 'Home of Mercy & Grace', we have two descent options. From here, we can drop steeply down **Caminho da Quinta Palmeira**, turning left onto **Rua da Banda de Além**; however, our route goes left here along the **Estrada de Misericórdia** road, for a gentler but longer descent.

Machico Marina

It's an easy walk above houses before we drop down to meet the new marina (Wp.8) where we go right along the promenade and into **Banda de Além** square by the bridge (Wp.9 76M), where we are close to a choice of bar/restaurants for refreshments in the centre of **Machico**.

18 THE OLD TRAIL TO CANIÇAL

There was a time before the ER-214 & VR1 roads when the main access to **Caniçal** was by donkey trail over the **Facho** ridge. When considered from standing in **Machico** it looks a daunting prospect, but with a little effort you can enjoy the wild landscapes between these two towns; our 'main route', starting from the **Caniçal** Tunnel entrance will however save you a considerable climb.

The old coastal path is now little walked and even less maintained; a shame, as it takes us through delightful countryside providing a refreshing change to forest and *levada* walking. Although rather rocky underfoot and overgrown in places, the route is quite discernable and easy to follow with the help of red markings and there are no precipitous sections.

Access by hire car or taxi: from **Machico**, follow the ER109 regional road towards **Caniçal**, parking close to the western entrance of the **Túnel do Caniçal**.

Alternative start from Machico: Follow directions (in reverse) for Walk 17 Pico do Facho - Machico (Wps. 9 - 2). Add 1 walker, 1 hour and 280 metres of ascent.

Access by bus: N°113 bus to **Túnel do Caniçal** entrance. Return on the N°113 bus from **Caniçal**. Alight at the western end of the tunnel.

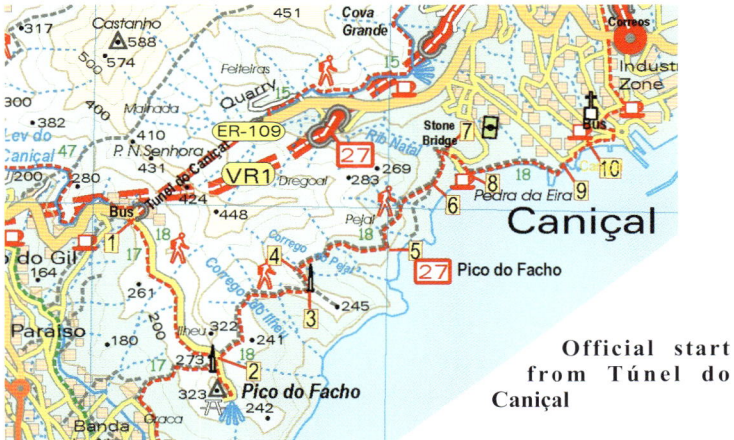

Official start from Túnel do Caniçal

Alighting from the N°113 bus at the start of the **Pico do Facho** road (Wp.1 0M), we stride up the tarmac leaving the houses behind, the gradient steepening to bring us to a water treatment station on our right, then passing below a cottage with a fire tender in its drive. After a 'croaking frog pond' in an old quarry, we continue to ascend again to meet the 'old coastal path', which crosses the road by a pylon (Wp.2 18M).

It's quite a slog up the road, but we recommend continuing the climb as far as the picnic area at **Pico do Facho** (refer to Walk 17), to enjoy the views down over **Machico** and the magnificent coastline along to the **São Lourenço** peninsula. Add around 20 minutes for this diversion as walk timings are for continuous walking from Wp.2.

The view from Pico do Facho after Wp.2

Our track gently descends northeast as it curves around the hillside to a junction. Ignoring a track off to the right, we curve north as the track narrows to a path above the steep **Corrego do Ilhéu** valley. The path drops down quite steeply before levelling out below traditional huts, then crossing the bowl of the valley above the steep cleft down to the sea. Ahead, a pylon surmounts a bare ridge and the trail starts climbing gently through tree-dotted slopes towards it, getting narrower and steeper as we push through tall heather to come onto the promontory beside the pylon (Wp.3 42M), an excellent if windy viewpoint over the rugged coastal landscape.

The rugged landscape

The path now has a discontinuity on the bare rock and it's easy to think the onward route is down the line of the ridge, but no! Facing the pylon, our correct route is left and behind us, dropping down beside a large rock along the northern side of the ridge. Our narrow, eroded path drops through mimosa trees to emerge between long abandoned terraces as we cross the valley's watercourse (Wp.4 49M). Stone walls guide us round a rocky ridge into a smaller, steeper valley notable for its rock walls.

Our path narrows before turning northeast towards **Caniçal** . When the route divides at a sheet of rock (with an old red paint waymark) we stay on the upper path for a gentle ascent along the top of a boulder wall.

Pride of Madeira

Coming alongside a rock outcrop the peninsula again comes into view; on rounding the outcrop we're looking down on **Caniçal** (Wp.5 74M). Our path runs inland below the outcrop before descending in zigzags, the route again confirmed by old red waymarks. The vegetation along the whole of this trail is typical of the island's coastal areas with Pride of Madeira, Prickly Pear and Globe Flower particularly dominant.

Over a stone ridge, our path now runs inland across grassy slopes to round a cleft slashed into the hillside before continuing down past old walls, coming high above the pebble beach at the mouth of the **Ribeira Natal** valley where the stone bridge comes into view (Wp.6 93M); if walking the route in reverse make sure you keep right at this point as continuing straight ahead leads to an impressive dead-end at the top of the cliffs.

The bridge at Wp.7

Our path becomes rockier, requiring concentration, as we drop towards the valley floor. A steep, scrambling descent finally brings us down to the stone bridge over the watercourse (Wp.7 103M).

Another few metres along, we meet a tarmac road serving the beach, where we turn right to stroll down to the mini yacht club (Wp.8 106M), then turning left, we pass along the beach-front promenade, which leads us to **Caniçal**'s road system (Wp.9). The new Whale Museum, the **Museu da Baleira**, a most impressive stone building, stands on the corner.

.. the lovely restored chapel ..

From the museum our trail takes us along the seafront passing beside the swimming pool as we head towards the harbour. Taking a left turn on **Rua da Calão**, running between a restaurant on the right and a garden area on the left where local men appear to spend the day playing cards under large palm trees, we have only a short climb to bring us into **Caniçal** square beside the lovely restored chapel. Crossing the square, we arrive on a new road where there's a taxi stand and bus stop on the left; going up the street straight ahead, we find more restaurants and bars for well-earned refreshment (Wp.10 121M).

Museu da Baleira -(The Whale Museum)
The museum is open daily from Tuesday to Sunday from 10.00 a.m. to 17.00 p.m. with the exception of:-
24, 25, 26 December
1 January
Easter Sunday.

There is a sliding scale for admission costs but in general it's around €10 for adults and €5 for children.

19 VEREDA DOS BALCÕES (PR11)

The viewing platform

One of three trails starting in **Ribeiro Frio**, we follow a beautiful scenic route to one of Madeira's most spectacular *miradouro* viewpoints. A short walk with good pathways and no precipitous drops, it's recommended for all. The best time to visit is during spring and summer when the flora is at its best and there's less chance of cloud invading the valley, blocking out the views.

Ribeiro Frio is one of the most popular tourist destinations on the island due to its stunning location below high peaks whilst nestling within the largest area of natural forest on the island. The centre boasts attractions including gift shops and restaurants as well as a trout farm and nature reserve, where many rare endemic forest plants are cultivated for display.

Access by hire car or taxi: take the ER103 to **Ribeiro Frio**. Car drivers can park near the bars, or lower down the road near the **Balcões** path, or at the picnic areas at the top end of the village.

Access by bus: bus N°s 56, 103 and 138 pass through the village; however, the service is limited.

From the settlement's two bars we walk down the road until it swings left; here an information board on the corner marks the start of our broad path (Wp.1 0M). Following **Levada Velha**, we head into the shady forest before meandering round the first valley head where we cross over a bridge.

Along this stretch the path winds away from the ER103 which can be seen descending the valley; looking eastwards, there's a rare opportunity to appreciate the scale and density of the *laurisilva*, its canopy rising over the eastern mountain slopes.

It's a wonderful location for escaping the heat of the summer and the vegetation is superb. Endemic species abound, including Rock Orchids (Orchis scopulorum) Madeira Stonecrop (Aichryson divaricatum) and Black Parsley (Melanoselinum decipiens) with its large trunk and umbel flower heads.

After ten minutes the route passes through a high rock cutting, then alongside rugged slopes, giving views down to **Faial**, before reaching the small log cabin of **Bar Flor da Selva** (Wp.2 18M) where you can stop for a drink or buy souvenirs, home made wines and plants.

The junction at Wp.3

The channel passes through another rock cutting before swinging left to arrive at a junction (Wp.3 23M) where 'Balcões' is signed along the right hand cobbled path.

Up to the viewing point

In two minutes we arrive at a spectacularly sited viewpoint standing on a rocky outcrop, paved and protected by fencing (Wp.4 30M). Mists permitting, we can look down into the **Metada Valley**, with **Penha d'Águia** to the north and the central mountain range to the west.

In the valley bottom, the generating station of **Fajã de Nogueira**, provides water and electricity for **Santana**, with **Levada Pico Ruivo** and **Levada da Serra** forming straight lines along the forest slopes. After soaking up these magnificent views, we return by the same route, arriving back at Wp.1 (60M).

Extension:
Once back in **Ribeiro Frio** we can take the path leading behind the new bar signed 'Portela', discovering many more endemic plants including the rare Yellow Foxglove (Isoplexis sceptrum) Madeira Betony (Teucrium abutiloides) and Madeira Elder. Other endemics can be seen at the **Posto Florestal Nature Reserve** adjacent to the **Fish Hatchery** (where rainbow trout are produced to replenish Madeira's watercourses) on the right of the road above the bars.

A number of rare species that are quite difficult to spot in their natural habitat within the forest are grown in the reserve; wild orchids Carrot Trees, Muschia wollastonii and Madeira Ironwort, making this extension a must for those interested in Madeira's flora.

20 SANTANA - PICO DAS PEDRAS to QUEIMADAS

A traditional A-framed cottage

The north coastal town of **Santana** comprises the parishes of **Arco de São Jorge**, **São Jorge**, **Ilha**, **Faial** and **São Roque do Faial**. An area rich in culture, it's famous for wine-making, traditional folklore and the pretty A-framed thatched cottages found scattered across the landscape. In addition it now hosts the new **Madeira Theme Park**.

Some of the best walking routes on the island are accessed from **Santana**, the pathway to **Pico Ruivo** (the highest peak at 1862m) is only around 5 kilometres up the ER218, plus there are a number of other high altitude routes and coastal pathways close by.

This trail takes us from **Rancho** in the **Pico das Pedras** forestry park to **Casa de Abrigo das Queimadas**, the most beautiful forestry house estate on the island and the starting point of the official **PR9 Levada do Caldeirão Verde**. A gentle stroll through a tranquil area of natural and exotic forest, it's extremely popular with visitors; it's also designated as a suitable trail for disabled and blind walkers.

At **Rancho** there's a snack bar as well as accommodation in the *colmos*, the traditional triangular shaped houses with thatched roofs.

The forest path from Pico das Pedras

Access by car:
Take the ER213 east from **Santana**, turning right after one kilometre onto the ER218, signed 'Achada do Teixeira'. The car park for **Rancho**, **Pico das Pedras** is located on the right of the road around 4 kilometres from the junction with the ER213. There is a large car park off the road with additional parking beside the snack bar.

Access by bus & taxi:
There is a regular bus service (Route N°s 56, 103 & 138) from **Funchal** to

Santana from where taxis are available to deliver you to the starting point at **Rancho** car park, **Pico das Pedras**.

When taking a taxi, make sure you also arrange your return journey with the driver - cost each way is approximately €15.

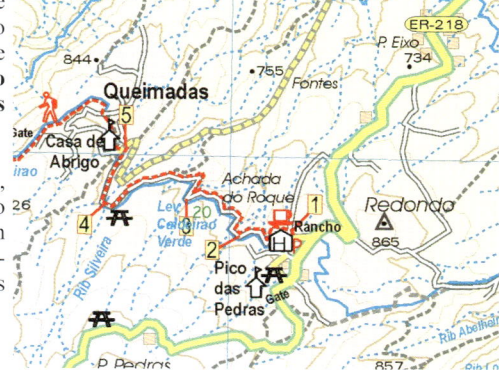

Leaving the car park (Wp.1 0M) and passing beside traditional houses, we enter the woodland, our pathway flanked with agapanthus and hydrangea and fenced throughout.

Soon we pick up the **Levada do Caldeirão Verde** running on our left and follow it upstream. A few minutes along it crosses over to the right (Wp.2 5M), from whereon the channel meanders back and forth across the broad tree-shaded trail. Deciduous oaks, beech and sycamore line our route alongside laurels and conifers, the latter including some splendid cedars - occasionally splashes of colour also appear from introduced camellias and azaleas.

Anemone-leaved crane's bill

We swing into a deeper valley, crossing the watercourse at its head (Wp.3 15M), our route soft and cushioned underfoot. Woodland flowers appear alongside the path; there are anemone-leaved crane's bill and Canary buttercups in abundance and the rare musschia wollastonii can also be spotted here.

Large patches of fungus grow on a maple tree to our left just before we arrive at a rushing stream, which we cross on a concrete bridge (Wp.4 30M). A few minutes later we leave the trail, stepping onto the cobbled access lane to **Parque das Queimadas** coming up on our right (Wp.5 35M). Crossing over, we enter into this wonderful estate situated

Canary buttercups

above the agricultural lands of **Santana**.

Casa de Abrigo das Queimadas

The forestry house, with original features of the typical houses in this region, has a marvellous thatched roof as does another smaller building close by and even the ducks have been provided with their own thatched houses on the banks of the two lovely ponds. It's now possible to have a drink and snack at **Casa das Queimadas**, which opened in October 2018.

The paved courtyard is surrounded by elegant parkland with excellent specimens of Japanese Cedars and European Beech as well as magnificent displays of rhododendrons.

You'll also find tame chaffinches hopping around the picnic area looking for scraps; it's a wonderful area and worthy of a visit in its own right.

Chaffinch

This is the end of our trail; from here we can either retrace our steps back to the starting point at **Rancho** (Wp.1 75M) or, extend the walk along **Levada do Caldeirão Verde (PR9)**. This well-known 6.5km trail (one way) is signed just beyond the house, taking us through the *laurisilva* into the interior. With spectacular views of the mountainous terrain along the way, it also passes through four tunnels before arriving at a huge basin with towering walls and here the **Caldeirão Verde** stream falls 100 metres into a lovely green lake. (See Walk! Madeira Volume 2, for the full walking notes on this route).

21 ABRIGO DO PASTOR CIRCULAR - POISO

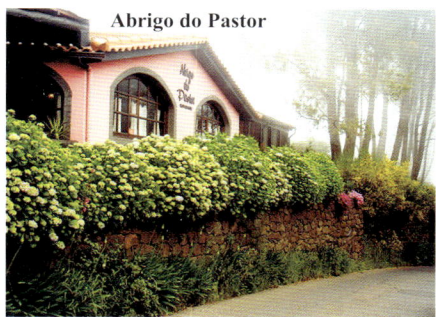

Abrigo do Pastor

This lovely circular walk starts and ends at **Abrigo do Pastor** (Shepherd's Rest), one of the best rural hostelries on the island. On walking into this charming establishment, you could be forgiven for thinking you are entering an English country pub, complete with open fire, wooden beams and a warm inviting atmosphere.

The walk takes us along ancient routes through forested vales and hills dotted with farming hamlets, before leading us into Madeira's main sheep farming area where unusual breeds, adorned with tinkling bells, roam in an idyllic setting of rolling moorland and deciduous woodland.

Access by car or taxi:
From **Camacha** follow the ER203 (Estrada Carreiras-Vale Paraiso) in the direction of **Poiso**. **Restaurante Abrigo do Pastor** is located approximately 3km from the **Camacha** junction on the right hand side of the road. Parking is available behind the restaurant.

We start the walk at the rear of the restaurant (Wp.1 0M) turning left into a cobbled lane a short distance from the car park (Wp.2 2M). Following the track, a narrow *levada* appears on our right as we descend to a rustic gate where we leave the track as it turns right.

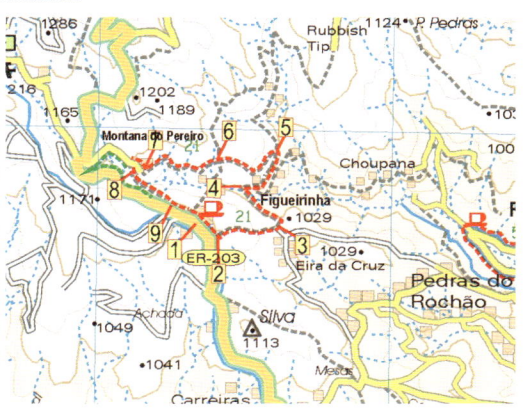

Through the gate, signed 'Vereda do Pedreira', our route then becomes a narrow path with a number of paved stepped sections, leading us down beside the fast flowing channel, and here the vast expanse of the farming valley opens up in front of us.

Passing beside agricultural plots and the first houses, the path soon turns left to meet a wide concrete track dropping deeper into the valley, eventually arriving at a junction with a vehicle track in the hamlet of **Figueirinha** (Wp.3 22M). Turning left here, and left again after 30 metres, we head along a wide concrete track into the woodland and, contouring around the valley side, we eventually cross over a bridge where a pink house sits on the hillside to our right (Wp.4 27M).

With lovely views all around and our route adorned with patches of white chrysanthemums (in summer), the track becomes a two-wheel earthen track after the second house, ascending to the next derelict house when it narrows into a single file path, soon arriving at a junction with a forest track (Wp.5 42M). Going right would lead us to the island's waste disposal plant, which can be seen on the hillside across the valley, but here we go left, circling through the pine and eucalyptus forest until we reach a rustic fence and gate (Wp.6 56M).

... sheep roam freely ...

Passing through the gate, the track continues as it now makes a steady climb and soon the sound of the tinkling sheep bells heralds our arrival at a smallholding with sheep pens and farm buildings (Wp.7 70M).

Throughout the year the sheep roam freely around and on each of our visits, large flocks have trundled across our path, plainly stirring recollections of life in Yorkshire. We've walked this route at different times of the year and unlike most of the island, the contrast of seasons here is quite striking.

Foxglove (Digitalis purpurea)

Holly

Deciduous species of beech, oak, willow and chestnut predominate and the landscape changes dramatically, with carpets of flowers below the fresh green leaves in spring and beautiful hues in autumn.

After the leaves have fallen, firs and pines take centre

stage, hollies are laden with berries and there's often even a scattering of snow to complete the winter scene; all in all, a most picturesque location.

At the annual sheep-shearing festival

This area also hosts Madeira's annual sheep shearing festival; a charming event with a brass band, folk dancers and food and beverages stalls, the surrounding moorland thronging with local families enjoying this cultural spectacle and well worth a visit for anyone on the island around the first week of June.

From the farm buildings, the road becomes tarred as it climbs up through the rocky terrain, arriving after 400 metres at a junction with the ER203 at **Montada do Pereiro**, one of the regional government's leisure and recreational facilities. This is an option for anyone wishing to extend the walk.

Our main route leaves the tarred road a short distance beyond the farm, where a left hand track drops down to cross over a bridge (Wp.8 75M) before turning left again to climb up through the forest.

From here we follow the earthen track, which becomes stony underfoot, as it veers right and then left and, after running parallel with the ER203 for a short distance, meets the regional road just above **Abrigo do Pastor** (Wp.9 90M).

This final section is under two hundred metres of road walking, while the alternative route via **Montada do Pereiro** is around one and half kilometers, the last 800 metres being along the road.

The forest track - final section to Abrigo do Pastor

Once back at the starting point, don't miss out on a visit to the restaurant. The food and ambience at this typical Portuguese establishment is excellent, reasonably priced and highly recommended.

22 SANTO DA SERRA - SERRADO DAS AMEIXIEIRAS - MADRE DE AGUA - CIRCULAR

Quinta da Serra exotic gardens

The green rolling hillsides and cooler climate of **Santo António da Serra** ensured it became a popular destination with the early English settlers, evidenced by a legacy of beautiful *quintas* around the village.

.. an avenue of camellias and azaleas ..

Quinta da Serra, just off the main square, is a fine example whose grounds are open to the public where you'll find magnificent trees and exotic plants, in particular an avenue of Camellias and Azaleas, so beautiful in early spring; deer, peacocks and waterfowl add to the charm of these gardens**.**

Another major attraction in the village and along the ER102 approach road is the Sunday market offering an assortment of local produce and crafts; it's extremely popular throughout the year and especially so at Christmas.

At the Christmas market

Our circular trail starts and ends close to the church and takes us along country lanes to the pretty hamlet of **Serrado das Ameixieiras**. Picking up a short section of **Levada dos Tornos**, we then visit the lovely chapel of **Capela Coração de Jesus** in **Sitio da Pereira** before dropping down an ancient pathway to return to **Ameixieiras**.

Indigenous species to look out for include fetid laurel, lily-of-the-valley, bilberry and heather, as well as the exotic flowering Himalayan ginger lily and banana maracuja, both making a splendid display throughout the summer.

* in Santo da Serra centre only

Access by hire car or taxi:
Leave the VR1 at either Junction 15 to follow VE5 to **Camacha** then continue along the ER102 to **Santo da Serra** or, leave the VR1 at Junction 21 following ER207 to **Santo da Serra**. Park in the square beside the church.

Access by bus:
SAM bus N°s 20 & 78 and Horários bus N°77 run services between **Funchal** and **Santo da Serra**.

Himalayan Ginger (Hedychium gardnerianum)

We leave the village (Wp.1) along a narrow lane opposite the church, the **Rua Padre João Pedro Gomes Henriques**, which we follow for a short distance. Ignoring a right turn signed 'No Entry', our route bears left along **Caminho da Pereira**. A few minutes later we cross the **Santo da Serra** bypass (Wp.2).

After a further 150 metres, at a fork in the road, we bear right, down the hill. Crossing a bridge over a stream, the stilt houses of **Quinta das Eiras** are visible to our right.

We continue our descent into the valley, crossing two more bridges before the lane starts climbing; we're following the boundary fencing of **Quinta Serrado das Ameixieiras**, soon reaching a crossroads (Wp.3 30M) to descend left down a cobbled track. 50 metres ahead we pass the main gates of the *quinta* and in another 100 metres, reach steps coming down on our right and the lower *quinta* gates on our left. We'll descend these steps on our return journey but for now we continue ahead.

Passing the first house on the right, a splendid old wine press appears also on the right. Just before reaching the next house we turn right down a narrow cobbled path, descending through agricultural plots (Wp.4 35M). Our path drops down the side of the valley through pine woods until it reaches the **Levada dos Tornos** (Wp.5 40M); we turn right to follow it up stream. This is the final section of an extremely long *levada* flowing across to the east from below the **Funchal Ecological Park**; though badly damaged in the Feb 2010 floods and still in a bad state of repair, there are no problems with this route.

Passing beside two small barns on our left, we continue along a very pretty section of forest; after negotiating a bridge (Wp.6 45M) below a waterfall and weir (the bridge damaged but passable with care), we arrive at a derelict house on our right (Wp.7 50M).

Capela Coração de Jesus

Five minutes ahead we emerge onto the tarred surface of **Caminho Madre de Agua** (Wp.8 55M); leaving the *levada* we turn right to follow the lane up hill for around 400 metres to reach a school in **Sitio da Pereira** (70M). Turning left here onto **Rua Mary Jane Wilson**, the chapel of **Capela Coração de Jesus** sits just below the road; during school hours it's possible to drop down the steps into the chapel gardens to view the lovely interior of the building. Also known as **Capela de Nossa Senhora da Saúde** (Our Lady of

Serrado das Ameixieiras

Health, built 1922), it was initially an orphanage for disadvantaged children, a legacy from the Franciscan charity founded by Mary Jane Wilson, a British Sister dedicated to the health, welfare and education of the ordinary people of the island.

Leaving **Sitio da Pereira** behind and passing a few houses on either side of the road, our route continues for another 700 metres to reach an electricity tower and the ancient cobbled track on our right of **Caminho Serrado das Ameixieiras** (Wp.9 90M), our route back to the hamlet of **Ameixieiras**.

We drop down this track before taking the first turn on the left, a narrow tarred driveway leading to two houses and a barn and after passing in front of the barn next to the agricultural plots we continue on a concrete path to reach the steps and *quinta* gate that we passed on our original descent into **Ameixieiras** (100M). Our trail turns left here to return by the same route to the centre of **Santo da Serra** (Wp.1 150M), but it's really worth turning right to spend a little time in this hamlet first, the houses and gardens are so pretty and the local people appear most happy to see visitors.

23 PICO DO AREEIRO - JUNCAL VIEWPOINT - NINHO DA MANTA

The route to Ruivo

Pico do Areeiro (1817m) is the start point for the **PR1 Vereda do Areeiro**, one of the island's most popular high altitude trails linking this peak with **Ruivo** (1862m), highest point on the island.

Echium candicans

A military radar station and reception centre dominate the area just below the summit, though this doesn't detract from the beauty of this spectacular mountain region. The reception centre houses a pleasant café and gift shop, as well as educational facilities.

Our short alternative trail provides an opportunity for everyone to enjoy walking a section of the **Areeiro** - **Ruivo** route as far as **Ninho da Manta**. It also takes in another short trail east, to the **Juncal** viewpoint overlooking the northern slopes and coastline.

Pico do Areeiro is an important area for flora and fauna and is the only known breeding site of the Zino's Petrel, Europe's rarest seabird and one of the rarest in the world; there are said to be between 65 and 80 pairs in this location. There's a wealth of rare high altitude flora too; in summer, Madeira thrift, chrysanthemums, hawkweed, kidney vetch, Echium candicans and rock mustard abound whilst rarer endemics such as Madeira eyebright, Madeira saxifrage, Madeira violets, and stonecrops cling to rock face crevices and ledges. The area sits close to the northern boundary of the **Funchal Ecological Park**, another important area of the national park; see footnote.

Access by car hire or taxi:
Follow the ER103 from **Funchal** via **Monte** and continue on to **Poiso**. At the road junction just beyond the **Abrigo do Poiso Restaurant**, go left on the ER202. It's around 7km to the car park at **Pico do Areeiro**.

Leaving the car park (Wp.1 0M) and passing around the left side of the building, we take steps up to the back terrace and follow the first section of the disabled access route to reach a paved pathway leading down to a turning circle at the gates to the radar station.

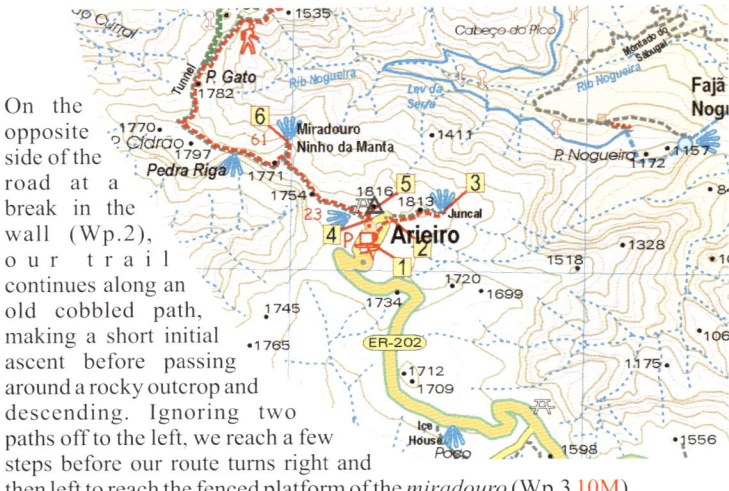

On the opposite side of the road at a break in the wall (Wp.2), our trail continues along an old cobbled path, making a short initial ascent before passing around a rocky outcrop and descending. Ignoring two paths off to the left, we reach a few steps before our route turns right and then left to reach the fenced platform of the *miradouro* (Wp.3 10M).

On the path to Juncal

From here there are fine views of the deep-forested valley of **Fajã da Nogueira** as well as the villages of **São Roque** and **Faial** and of **Penha de Águia** (Eagle Rock) on the north coast. The hydropower station at **Fajã da Nogueira** can be seen deep in the valley, as can the *levadas* that feed the station which provides power for the northern settlements.

Ninho da Manta

Retracing our steps and heading back towards the summit of **Areeiro**, the trail picks up the disabled access as it zig-zags up to a junction; the path to **Ninho da Manta** (Wp.4 30M) leads off left here, steps to the peak go right.

At the top of the steps go left to follow a circular path clockwise, soon taking another short flight of steps to the summit (Wp.5 35M). After soaking up the magnificent views we return to Wp.4 to follow the paved walkway of **PR1** across the narrow saddle of a vast rocky area, our path making a steep descent down many steps before reaching a wide grassy area. There are magnificent views all around with the main route to **Ruivo** seen continuing along the mountain range below **Pico das Torrres**. From the grassy area there's a short ascent before dropping again to the foot of a huge rocky outcrop on top of which sits the **Ninho da Manta** *miradouro*. Climbing steps beside the rock face, the **PR1** trail to **Ruivo** ascends left, while our trail turns right to reach the viewpoint (Wp.6 60M). We retrace our steps back to the car park (Wp.1 90M).

As there's no public transport to **Pico do Areeiro** you'll be travelling by hire car, taxi or tour bus. Whichever mode of transport you choose, try to arrange to stop at the **Poço da Neve** (Snow House) on your return journey. Also known as the **Ice House**, it is situated on the right of the ER202 1½km from the summit car park. Built by Madeiran stonemasons and financed by an Italian ice-cream maker, the **Ice**

Poço da Neve

A section of the new road

House provided ice for hospitals and **Reid's Hotel** from 1813 until the end of the 19th century. Access to this amazing monument is by a narrow paved path leading from the road across the moorland. Also of interest, close to the Ice House, is a new

amazing viewing platforms along the new road

16 km road heading down the mountains to reach **Eira do Serrado** above **Curral das Freiras**. If you have the transport we recommend you take this route back to your base. It's an amazing experience you won't forget. The road, built mainly with EU money, opened in 2012, providing essential access to mountainous areas susceptible to fire damage.

Funchal Ecological Park
The **Ice House** stands on the northern boundary of the **Funchal Ecological Park**, which occupies an area of around 1000 hectares, extending from the forested areas above **Funchal** to **Pico Areeiro**. Sadly, the park suffered severe damage in the August 2010 fires when 95% of its area was affected.

The area is recovering well although the restoration programme for tree clearance and replanting will take a number of years. Unfortunately some of the signed walking routes and the bird-watching routes were also destroyed in the fires and we understand that it will be another two or three years before these are reinstated. Happily however, one walking trail survived and is included in this publication (See Walk 8 Ecological Park to Monte). The park is popular with visitors, offering the **Reception and Information Centre** at **Ribeira das Cales** where there's a café and a nursery raising endemic species for the replanting programme. Picnic, barbeque and recreational facilities throughout the park are popular with families all year round.

24 LEVADA DO FURADO - (PR10) RIBEIRO FRIO TO PORTELA

Ribeiro Frio nestles below the high peaks within the largest area of natural forest on the island. The centre boasts many attractions including a gift shop, restaurants and a trout farm and nature reserve and as well as the starting point for this popular walk to **Portela**, it's also the starting point for Walk 19 **Vereda dos Balcões**.

The first section of the trail passes through an exceptional area of *laurisilva*; sub-tropical forest where wild flowers flourish beneath the tree canopy, bringing colour and contrast. There are impressive rock cuttings and a wonderful series of tunnels and arches at **Cabeço Furado** - no torch required. Newly constructed along its whole length with sturdy safety fencing erected on all necessary sections, makes this an almost vertigo-free route.

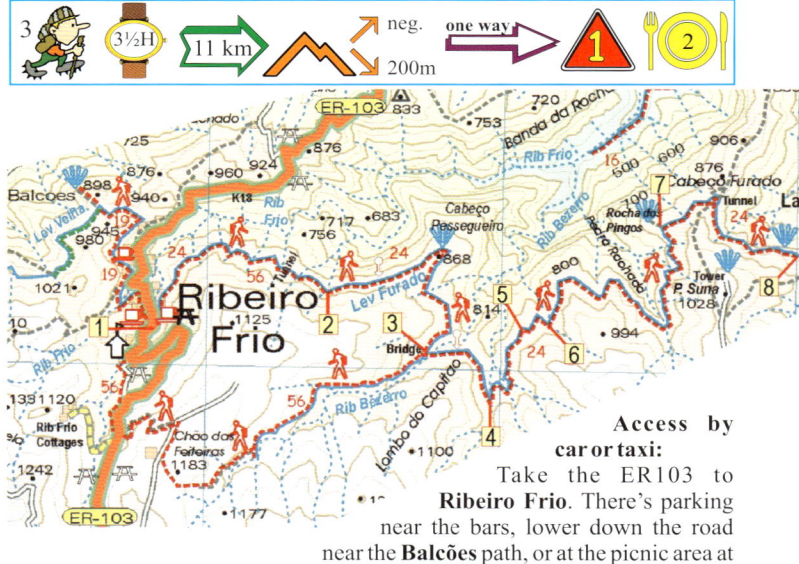

Access by car or taxi:
Take the ER103 to **Ribeiro Frio**. There's parking near the bars, lower down the road near the **Balcões** path, or at the picnic area at the top end of the village. Taxis are available in **Portela** for your return to **Ribeiro Frio**. See final paragraph for details.

Access by bus:
Horários Interurban bus Nºs 56, 103 & 138 provide a limited daily service between **Funchal** & **Santana**, passing through **Ribeiro Frio**. Return from **Portela** on SAM bus Nºs 20, 53 or 78 (limited service) via **Machico** to **Funchal**. Currently the bus times for these services are compatible with the one-way trail but do arm yourself with an up to date timetable before setting out. There is no bus service from **Portela** back to **Ribeiro Frio**.

Starting below the bars (Wp.1) a fingerpost directs us down a paved pathway where we cross a bridge and turn left, passing an information panel. Following the newly laid path along the riverbank, **Levada Furado** soon appears on our right, the path then veering right to enter the forest. A few

The rock cutting before Wp.2

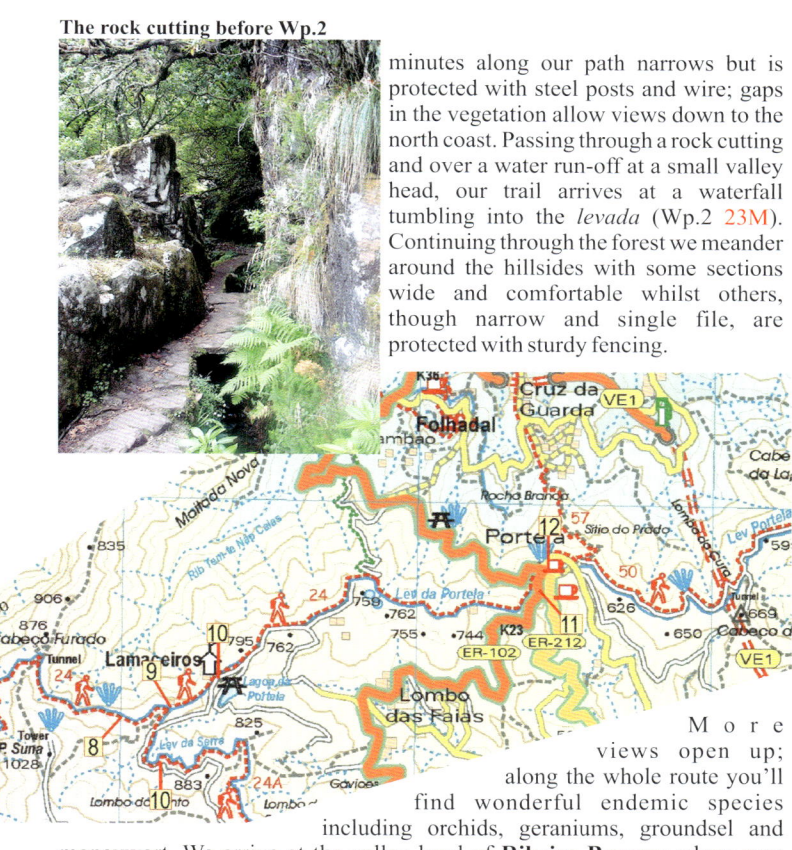

minutes along our path narrows but is protected with steel posts and wire; gaps in the vegetation allow views down to the north coast. Passing through a rock cutting and over a water run-off at a small valley head, our trail arrives at a waterfall tumbling into the *levada* (Wp.2 23M). Continuing through the forest we meander around the hillsides with some sections wide and comfortable whilst others, though narrow and single file, are protected with sturdy fencing.

More views open up; along the whole route you'll find wonderful endemic species including orchids, geraniums, groundsel and moneywort. We arrive at the valley head of **Ribeira Bezerro** where new channels feed into the *levada* and sluice gates appear (Wp.3 52M). The route now turns left to cross the stream on a concrete bridge where many finches flit around, so tame and used to walkers, they'll take food from your hand. Around fifteen minutes from the bridge the *levada* passes alongside the rock face with dripping water and views across the tree canopy. We reach the first of a number of detours where steps lead down left to cross the streams rising again on the other side (Wp.4 67M). (Care must be taken here to spot the fencing line down the steps, as the channel shoulder suddenly becomes a ledge. Turn back immediately if you miss the fencing as the shoulder is unsafe from this point).

At this first detour, there is a small pool below the channel and, if visiting during July and August, look out for the Yellow Foxglove (Isoplexis sceptrum), a rare endemic. Climbing steps we pass through the first of a number of rock cuttings (Wp.5 85M) where the path squeezes through on paved sections; another few minutes along a pretty shrine stands behind the channel (Wp.6 88M). The *levada* runs into a tunnel, necessitating a detour on a lower path and a few minutes later, at a valley head, we leave the channel again on another detour. With more openings in the vegetation looking down on **Faial** and **São Roque**, the route turns sharp right to negotiate a huge and impressive rock cutting. We arrive at a short side path on our left (Wp.7 140M) offering an excellent viewpoint on the edge of the promontory; a good place to take a short break before reaching an amazing section of the trail. At **Cabeço Furado** the *levada* clings to the valley side, passing along a section of narrow ledges through short tunnels. This area is newly protected with posts and wire; it's exhilarating though care is needed especially when wet underfoot. Emerging from the tunnels (Wp.8 150M) our trail heads for the **Lamaceiros** water house, set in a clearing. Passing in front of the building our route turns right to reach a junction of paths and signposts (Wp.9 155M). We turn left down the wide track signed 'Portela'; the route right along the forest track leads to **Santo da Serra** whilst the path sharp right heads up to **Pico do Suna**. A few metres along our route veers off left down a semi-stepped path alongside the **Levada do Portela**. At the bottom of the descent we enter the attractive gardens of the **Lamaceiros** forestry house (Wp.10 160M).

The stairway to the *miradouro*

On the right of the garden, steps lead down to a *miradouro* looking across **Lagoa da Portela**, the newly created reservoir formed in Madeira's largest volcanic crater; it's an impressive sight and if you have time, worth

Superb views from the belvedere

dropping down the new rustic stairway for a closer look. Leaving the gardens, we follow the forest road downhill passing the new reservoir road on our right before reaching a junction where our route is signed off left (PR10 Portela - 1.7km).

Now in open sunshine, we pass beside the large, fenced agricultural development of **Lombo dos Faias** on our right with spectacular views of **Porto da Cruz** to our left. At a derelict water house the *levada* divides; a narrow channel shooting left downhill; we follow this on a log-stepped descent.

Entering an area of mature pines and a hedge of Madeira Juniper, we drop down a flight of earthen steps to arrive on the ER102 road beside an information panel (Wp.11 205M). Turning left here, passing a new viewing platform with souvenir and flower stalls, our trail ends at the **Portela** belvedere beside the **Miradouro da Portela Restaurante** where there are superb views down to **Porto Cruz** and **Eagle Rock** (Wp.12 210M).

If you're traveling back by bus, continue 150 metres downhill to the bus stop opposite the **Portela A Vista** bar. Taxis are always available around the viewpoints to take you back to **Ribeira Frio**. The fare is €25 weekdays €30 weekends. You could suggest to others that you share a taxi to reduce costs.

24A LEVADA DO FURADO - RIBEIRO FRIO TO SANTO DA SERRA

As an alternative to our walk 24 ending in **Portela**, this trail covers the first exciting eight kilometres of **PR10 Levada do Furado** as far as **Lamaceiros**, where we then head off on our final section to **Santo da Serra**.

Both routes are fine walking trails, and each of the final destinations is worthy of a visit. However, the route to **Santo da Serra** is a longer trail and misses out on **Portela**'s spectacular views but we believe that this option may be popular for anyone staying in or around **Santa da Serra** or for those relying on the bus service back to **Funchal**; **Santo da Serra** offering one additional service on bus route 77 providing a little more flexibility with bus time tables. Car drivers will need to take a taxi back to **Ribeiro Frio**, as there is no return bus service from either of these locations. (See Walk 24 for taxi details).

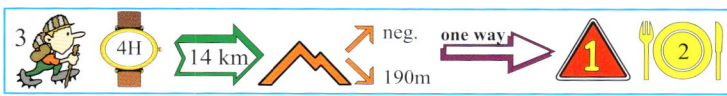

Access by bus:
Horários Interurban bus Nºs 56, 103 & 138 provide a limited daily service between **Funchal** & **Santana**, passing through **Ribeiro Frio**. From **Santo da Serra**, we return to **Funchal** on SAM bus Nºs 20 & 77 service; check the departure times as services are approximately 2 hourly. There is no bus service from **Santa da Serra** back to **Ribeiro Frio**.

Access by hire car or taxi:
Please follow the directions for Walk 24 to **Ribeiro Frio**.

For this option we leave **Ribeiro Frio** following the main route as far as the junction of paths beyond **Lamaceiros** water house (Wp.9 155M), where we follow the wide woodland pathway straight ahead alongside the reconstructed **Levada da Serra do Faial**.

Madeira Walks 1

From this point on the vegetation changes from the natural forest to coniferous where we find magnificent specimens of Cedar, Juniper and Cypress along the route. In a few minutes the channel veers off right to round a small valley head; here a short detour leaves the *levada* to cross over the stream bed, reconnecting with the channel on the opposite side (Wp.10 162M). Following left, our route soon crosses over a forest track. A short distance ahead, the channel goes through a small tunnel with the path rising above it.

Santo da Serra water house

In fifteen more minutes there's another detour below the channel making a short descent into the woodland before ascending back to meet the *levada*. We arrive at the **Santo da Serra** water house (Wp.11 196M), a similar structure to the last one though with unique, amazing tree specimens beside the house.

Just beyond the building, a small track drops down left to reach a junction with the main forest track, our route to **Santo da Serra**. This can easily be missed, but by bearing right after the water house and continuing along the now disused *levada*, the channel crosses this main track and turning left here, the junction with the alternative route is found a few metres down the hill. Dropping down the forest track through mixed woodland where mimosa and maple dominate, the first house appears and the track becomes tarred. Thirty minutes from the water house, we reach the ER102 on the outskirts of **Santo da Serra** (Wp.12 225M).

Turning right and heading down the road, we reach a roundabout and going left, follow the ER207 to the church and the town centre where taxis and buses are available (Wp.13 240M); call local taxi driver Duarte on 962028021.

25 RABAÇAL: LEVADA DO RISCO (PR6.1)

This short forest walk to an impressive waterfall is a must for anyone wanting to discover Madeira's interior without too much exertion. At **Risco**, the **Ribeira Grande** plunges 100 metres down a sheer rock face from **Lagoa do Vento**, before falling a further 100 metres down to **Levada das 25 Fontes** and then continuing into the **Ribeira da Janela** valley to the northwest. The route to this beauty spot is well-trodden and a favourite amongst visitors to the island, so whatever time of year you visit, you won't be alone. Also not to be missed, is the **Rabaçal Nature Spot Café**, opened in 2018, it's a real gem, serving home made food in a fabulous location.

Access by car:
The viewpoint, lies at 1290 m above sea level and is situated on the ER105 approximately 4.5 km west of the **Paúl da Serra** crossroads. A shuttle bus connecting the car park with the Forestry Post operates daily from 9.30 a.m. until 6.30 p.m (except Christmas Day and New Year's Day) and runs at approximately 20 minute intervals. Our choice for this otherwise short route is to go on foot, leaving the road barrier on the right of the car park (Wp.1 0M) and descending the tarred road leading down to the Forestry Post.

The descent to Rabaçal Forestry Post

The road drops through the lower heath forest, soon crossing **Ribeira do Alecrim** which flows down from **Paul da Serra** plateau, forming a pretty roadside pool (Wp.2 10M). The vegetation on the descent is predominantly heather and bilberry interspersed with broom and the occasional laurel, together creating a reasonably low, yet extremely dense forested area. This initial descent takes around 25 minutes

The fingerpost at Wp.6

On reaching the Forestry Post (Wp.3 25M) we descend a short flight of steps to the side of the building, turning immediately right to drop down a path into the forest to reach a junction with a dirt track alongside **Levada do Risco** (Wp.4 30M). Going right again, we soon meet another track coming down from the right (Wp.5 35M); this is our return route, but for now we continue to follow the channel against the water flow, passing a finger post on our left signed 'Levada das 25 Fontes' (Wp.6 40M). Ignoring this, we carry on alongside the channel, the damp conditions ideal for numerous varieties of

Rabaçal Nature Spot Café

ferns, mosses and grasses. In spring or summer we can expect to see a number of endemic species including the wonderful Shrubby Sow Thistle, Anemone-Leaved Cranes-Bill, Madeira Orchids, Canary Buttercups and Madeira Moneywort. This section offers beautiful views down the **Ribeira da Janela** valley with **Levada das 25 Fontes** and **Levada da Rocha Vermelha** clearly visible in the valley below. Twenty minutes after the sign, we arrive in the semi-circular basin of **Risco** waterfall to admire this spectacular natural landmark from the viewpoint (Wp.7 60M). The waterfall crashes down the volcanic rock face, disappearing from view into the valley far below.

.. the waterfall crashes down ..

From this point the *levada* shoulder is no longer passable, but can be seen as it tunnels into the rock, leading behind the waterfall and then on through further tunnels around the wooded rock face. Impressive throughout the year, the waterfall is particularly spectacular in winter, following heavy rain. The pathway along the whole route is protected with rustic fencing on the exposed sections and, approaching the waterfall viewpoint, steel posts and fencing have been added.

Returning to our starting point, we now retrace our steps to the fork where the *levada* flows off to our right and from here continue on the higher path back to the Forestry Post (Wp.3 90M) where we can enjoy refreshments at the stylish Nature Spot Café before picking up the shuttle bus; if you wish to walk back to the car park, add 1.5km to your distance (approximately 30 minutes, climbing 220m).

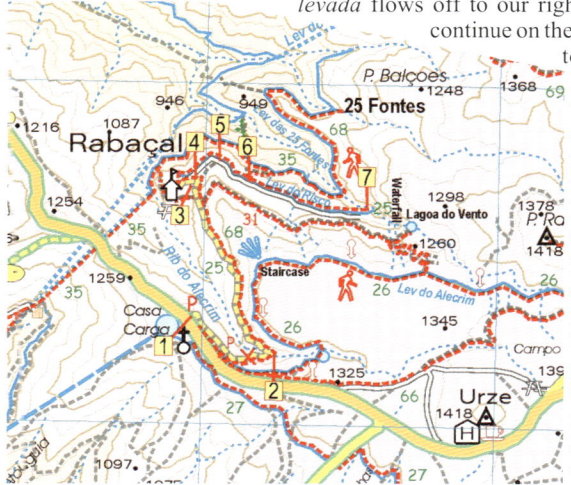

26 RABAÇAL: RIBEIRA GRANDE

At the top of the **Rabaçal** access road is one of the island's newest water channels, **Levada do Alecrim**, completed in 1961, provides access to a spectacular gorge with an impressive waterfall and clear blue pool, perfect for picnics, feeding the trout or swimming during the warmer months.

Along the Levada do Alecrím

Clearly visible from the car park, the trail follows an almost straight line through the forest and maintains height along the contours of the hillside, taking in a lovely water stairway along its route. It's an easy walk with the precipitous sections now protected with fencing, making it safe for everyone,

Access by hire car or taxi: for directions to **Rabaçal** car park and viewpoint follow Walk 25, turning into the access road and parking on the grass below the junction.

From the road barrier, our well-trodden path leads off right (Wp.1 0M); we follow it for 50 metres before meeting the *levada* path, then follow this left (Wp.2 2M).

Ribeira da Janela Valley

The channel shoulder provides a comfortable although quite stony path, framed by tree heather which unfortunately obscures most of the views along the initial section until the *levada* sweeps north-west, when breaks in the vegetation provide wonderful views down the valley.

Heading off against the water flow, we pass occasional slabs bridging the channel, one of which leads to a weather station, before passing a water collection pool teeming with trout (Wp.3 11M) beside the **Ribeira do Alecrím**, its waters diverted into the pool. Across the river, our easy path continues past a spring before coming to a viewpoint, which overlooks our start point.

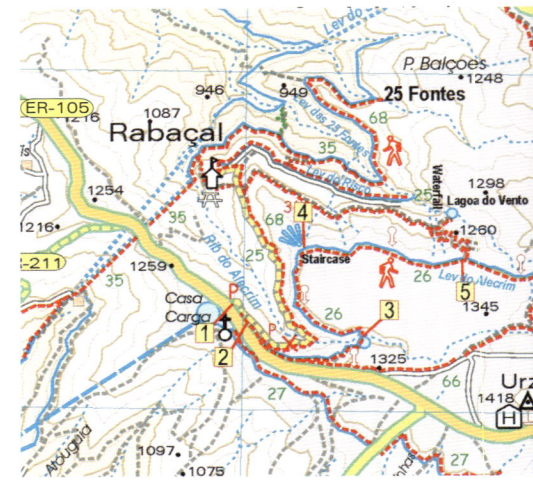

A little further along, our trail passes through a couple of rock cuttings where there are a number of precipitous sections, but the path is quite wide and the lush vegetation gives a sense of security.

Around the half way point we reach a spectacular water stairway (Wp.4 22M) where the *levada* rushes down a steep chute from its higher level. After climbing to the top we are rewarded with further magnificent views down the valley.

... a spectacular water stairway ...

The *levada* above the stairway narrows noticeably from this point, as we curve towards the **Ribeira Grande** gorge, crossing another short unprotected section before the easy walking continues.

The Ribeira Grande waterfall

From here we have views of the gentle rolling hilltops which rise above the tree line changing colour dramatically with the seasons. If you're extremely observant along this section, you may spot the junction with our Walk 65 (Volume 2) to **Lagoa do Vento**, the path descending from the channel shoulder to the forest below (Wp.5 44M).

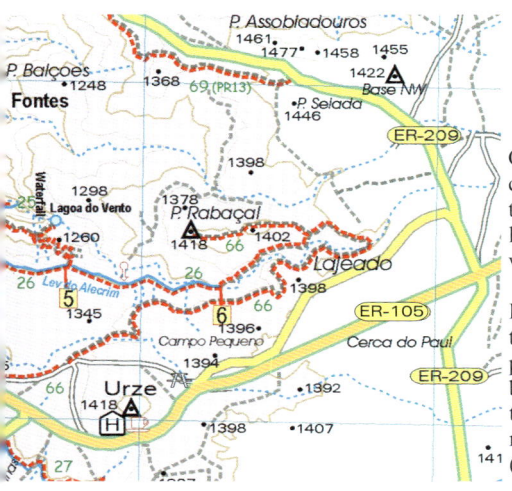

Continuing, we soon meet tiny channels and streams feeding the *levada* and five minutes later, cross a water runoff where care is needed.

Looking down to our left at this point, we see a large green pool below us and rounding a bend, we eventually arrive at the beautiful gorge, pool and river bed of **Ribeira Grande** (Wp.6 55M).

Take time to relax and absorb the experience before retracing your steps back to the car park (Wp.1 110M).

Ribeira Grande, also known as **Ribeira Lajeado**, cascades down from **Pico Rabaçal** and the area of **Lajeado**. From this point the river is referred to as **Ribeira Grande** until it reaches the valley floor and feeds into the **Ribeira da Janela** heading north.

27 LEVADA DO PAÚL - CRISTO REI TO FÁTIMA CHAPEL, RABAÇAL

The narrow channel of **Levada do Paúl** flows along open moorland where pale green hills sweep away below us giving way to darker forested areas. On clear days there are wonderful views of the southern coastline with **Achada de Santo Antão** at **Arco da Calheta** first in view.

.. cattle roam freely ..

Southern views

Undoubtedly we'll meet other walkers as we progress along this well-trodden route; it's also a grazing area for the cattle that roam freely around these hillsides so don't be surprised to find them on the pathway; fortunately, they're not obstructive so it's simply a matter of being patient and allowing them to pass.

Access by car or taxi:
Follow the ER105 from the **Encumeada** pass to the **Paúl da Serra** crossroads, turning left onto the ER209. After a further 3 kms, turn right into the car park beside the **Cristo Rei** statue.

Leaving the car park, we follow the ER209 downhill for a short distance to where the channel crosses under the road just after a right hand bend. Here we turn right, following the *levada* downstream (Wp.1 0M).

Our route immediately heads into the first valley and with

100 Madeira Walks 1

wind turbines above us, we round its head to ford a pretty stream on stepping-stones (Wp.2 10M). The river tumbles down its rocky bed before dropping into a small gorge to our left. Note that cattle gates have been erected between Wps. 1&2, though there is no problem with access.

A few minutes along, we arrive at the second waterfall (Wp.3 30M), after which the terrain becomes much rockier, the contrasts of this pleasant moorland changing with the seasons, the bright green bracken and yellow broom and gorse of spring and summer, autumn colours prevailing in winter.

The third waterfall - a lovely setting for lunch

The third waterfall (Wp.4 40M) with its little weir and clear pool provides a lovely setting for a rest or lunch.

After leaving this pretty spot and crossing over a moorland track (Wp.5 50M), we reach intriguing caves dug into the rocky hillside (Wp.6 70M), beyond which the *levada* becomes a corridor between tall broom before snaking once again round open hillside, arriving at the new regional road leading down to **Arco da Calheta** (Wp.7 80M).

Intriguing caves along the *levada*

N.B. This route is currently closed from (Wp7) where the channel crosses the regional road until it reaches the chapel of Nossa Senhora de Fátima and the Rabaçal car park on the ER105 at (Wp.8). The section of the route between these waypoints is due to be reopened in 2020. As an temporary alternative, follow the road right for 300m before turning left onto the ER105 to reach Rabaçal.

Another twenty minutes brings us alongside the pretty chapel of **Nossa Senhora de Fátima** and, just to the left, a reservoir that feeds the hydropower station in **Calheta**; we climb a path beside this to cross over to the **Rabaçal** *miradouro* and car park (Wp.8 105M).

From here, we turn around, retracing our steps back to the starting point, enjoying the different perspectives from this direction.

1.7 kilometres east of the car park, you'll find the **Jungle Rain** bar, restaurant and tourist shop, a good place to visit and watch the world go by. We rejoin our outward route by walking back (600 metres) towards **Rabaçal** to drop down the **Arco** road to meet the water channel at Wp.7.

Cristo Rei

Cristo Rei Statue
The white marble statue of **Cristo Rei** was erected in 1962. Also known as **Nosso Senhor da Montanha** (Our Lord of the Mountain) the area is surrounded by trees and terracing, creating a little oasis in this moorland area.

Below the statue stands a large arch, other sculptures and a spring, plus a number of stone plinths inscribed with religious proverbs.

28 AROUND FANAL

The Fanal mountain area

The unique **Fanal** woods and mountains around the forestry post are a magnet for family picnics, barbecues and recreation at weekends and holiday times. The area surrounding the house could be described as parkland, its pastures populated with groves of centuries-old Madeira laurels; (Fetid Laurel or Til tree *Ocotea foetens*) which have grown to enormous proportions with amazing art forms.

This short circular taking in the final section of **PR13 Vereda do Fanal** is an ideal taster for exploring this beautiful area.

Fanal woods

It also links well with two more routes through the **Fanal** forests; Walk 32 **Levada dos Cedros** (PR14) and Walk 33 **Vereda da Ribeira da Janela** (**PR15**), make a continuous route from the forestry house to the terraced agricultural parish of **Ribeira da Janela**.

* + extensions

Access by car or taxi:
Follow the ER105 to the **Paúl da Serra** crossroads taking the ER209 signed 'Fanal & Ribeira da Janela'. The Forestry Post is situated on the right hand side of the road, approximately 8.3kms from the junction.

Taking steps on the right of the forestry house (Wp.1 0M) our trail heads up to the flagpoles, going straight ahead before descending to a tarmac road coming up from the forestry driveway. Veering left, the road becomes an earthen track leading us to a wide-open expanse of pastureland criss-crossed with several other tracks.

Keeping straight ahead, we follow the central track towards a thicket of trees. As our route ascends, a fingerpost eventually appears indicating 'Fanal 2.2 km', directing us left down a narrow pathway through the vegetation (Wp.2 20M). From this point on the route follows the final section of **Vereda da Fanal**, the **PR13** official walking route.

There's a short detour from this junction taking us to a lovely *miradouro* overlooking **Chão da Ribeira da Seixal**; continue up the track for a further five minutes taking a left turn onto the viewing platform. Allow around fifteen minutes for this extension. Back on our route at the 'Fanal 2.2 km' sign, we descend the narrow pathway through the vegetation to

Miradouro above **Chão da Ribeira da Seixal**

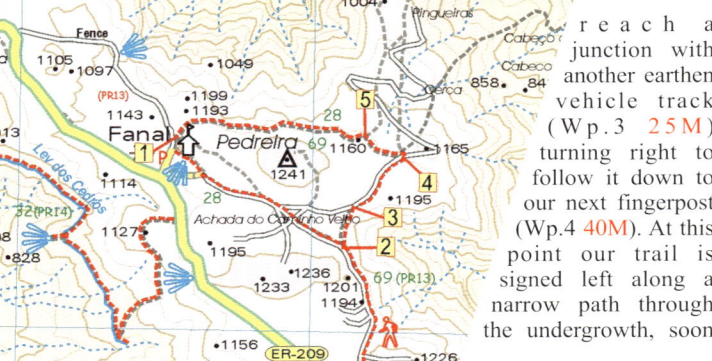

reach a junction with another earthen vehicle track (Wp.3 25M) turning right to follow it down to our next fingerpost (Wp.4 40M). At this point our trail is signed left along a narrow path through the undergrowth, soon

Approaching the knoll

reaching an old A-framed barn almost hidden in the trees a short distance ahead; another fingerpost (Wp.5 50M) directs us left again to begin a short ascent into the forest. Many more of the ancient Fetid Laurels can be seen along this section - quite spectacular! Endemic species of orchid and Mandon's chrysanthemum can also be seen in summer. With stunning views down to the northern coastal areas, our path eventually emerges onto a grassy plateau where a splendid high knoll ahead of us dominates the scene, the natural forest sweeping down below us.

Walking through carpets of flowers whilst passing beside two field code markers, our route veers off left along a narrow path before dropping down a logged stairway into the **Fanal** picnic area in the forestry post woodland (Wp.1 75M).

This is the end of the trail, but allow time here to roam around this charming area before descending the driveway to reach the regional road. Another official information panel close to the gateway gives the phone number of a local taxi service (or see Appendix A for alternative taxi numbers) and for anyone with surplus energy, links with other routes.

29 CRISTO REI - LEVADA DA BICA DA CANA

Levada da Bica da Cana

Another route from **Cristo Rei**, this time taking us in an easterly direction following **Levada da Bica da Cana**.

It's an exhilarating walk along this narrow channel which eventually leads us into the mountains, yet the terrain is comfortable and the views just get better and better as you progress along.

In the past, it was possible to combine this trail with Walk 3, to make a continuous route via **Cascalho** to **Boca da Encumeada**; unfortunately the route was closed following floods in 2010. (See footnote for details)

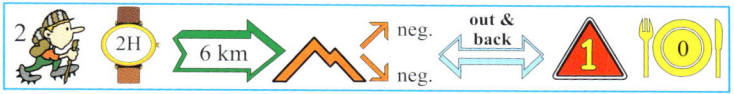

Access by car or taxi:
Follow the ER105 from the **Encumeada p**ass to the **Paúl da Serra** crossroads turning left onto the ER209. After a further 3 kms, turn right into the car park beside the **Cristo Rei** statue or park on the roadside a little further down.

Dropping down the road from the statue (Wp.1 0M), **Levada do Paúl** crosses in front of an old water house standing on our left, before disappearing under the road on its route to **Rabaçal**. We follow the channel east passing in front of the house and through a rock cutting to arrive at a stream bed. Here the two

channels separate and we now follow **Levada da Bica da Cana** upstream.

Moving along the clay and grass path where gorse and broom abound, another channel soon appears crossing diagonally before continuing down the hillside; just beyond, we reach a valley head crossing over a water run-off (Wp.2 10M). Our path snakes along the moorland, occasionally crossing small becks and springs and as we stroll along we take in the superb views down to the southern villages and coastline.

The junction with the cobbled lane

Rounding the next hillside, deep slopes appear on our right with coniferous forest lying in the valley bottom and, along this barren ridge, we arrive at a spot ideal for a picnic where a huge pine stands in isolation, quite striking (Wp.3 22M). Three minutes ahead we reach a T-junction with a cobbled lane coming down from the left and descending into the valley on our right (Wp.4 25M).

On the opposite side of the track the *levada* can be seen coursing down a slope; we cross the track and ascend to a cairn and a magnificent viewpoint at the top of the slope (Wp.5 29M).

Endemic sow thistles

We are now standing on a mountain pass high above the **Ponta da Sol** valley and are looking across to the **Encumeada** pass; it's spectacular!

Our route turns left and passes over a stile before continuing along the hillside. The path becomes quite wet and muddy in places and the shoulder narrows, though there's lots of vegetation for protection.

Levada da Bica da Cana

Endemic giant sow thistles grow along this section flowering during the summer months. The route becomes more beautiful and remote as we continue deeper into the valley.

The rocky section

Towards the end we must negotiate a couple of narrow and exposed sections of shoulder, also hampered by overhanging rock; nevertheless these short sections are passable with care and we soon continue again along the grassy pathway.

As we approach the valley head, an earthen track can be seen descending the valley with the narrow channel climbing up the hillside ahead. The track is the route down to **Cascalho**; the channel comes down the hillside bringing the waters of *levada* **Bica da Cana** from their source.

We arrive at the T-junction and cross the track to continue following the *levada* on the opposite side (Wp.6 52M).

The next section is narrow and we negotiate a waterfall bursting over the *levada*, but the shoulder is well constructed and the surface even, so we can easily pass along for another few minutes until the channel veers left (Wp.7 57M). At this point we turn around and retrace out steps back to **Cristo Rei** (Wp.1 120M).

Continuous route via Cascalho and Boca da Encumeada (Total route 12km - 4 hrs one-way)

The track drops down the valley on a 350 metre descent, taking you to the source of the **Ponta do Sol** river; here waterfalls cascade down over a rock-walled amphitheatre. It's quite an exposed area but it is fenced and passable with care. En-route this trail passes through three tunnels, the longest of which is around 3 km and takes 1 hour to negotiate.

Important Note:
This route was still closed when last researched in November 2018 but will hopefully reopen at some point in the future. Anyone interested in walking this continuous trail should check with the tourist offices to ascertain the status before setting out.

30 VEREDA DO CHÃO DOS LOUROS CIRCULAR - SÃO VICENTE VALLEY (PR22)

A newly introduced PR circular on the northern slopes below **Encumeada**, this trail moves through the *laurisilva* surrounding the **Chão dos Louros Park**, providing a tranquil and scenic journey where we can enjoy nature. The route intersects with (**PR21 Caminho do Norte**), another new official walking trail from **Encumeada Pass** to **Ribeira Grande**, above **São Vicente**.

A view from the park

The park occupies a beautiful area below the eastern mountain range offering great views of the peaks on clear days. Within the boundaries are picnic tables, barbeques, recreational facilities and toilets; it's not surprising that it's an extremely popular location with Madeiran families at weekends and holiday times.

Access by hire car or taxi:
From **Ribeira Brava** follow the VE4 turning left on to the ER105 to **Encumeada Pass**. Turn right onto the ER228 signed **São Vicente**, **Chão dos Louros Park** is situated around 1.2 km ahead on the right hand side of the road.

Access by bus:
Not suitable for bus access.

The information board for this trail is situated inside the park close to the road (Wp.1 0M) and whilst it's worth exploring the park at this point, the actual walk starts a little higher up on the opposite side of the road where a finger post (Wp.2 2M) directs us up a narrow track into the forest.

Looking down to São Vicente

The trail meanders and zigzags climbing up through the *laurisilva* allowing occasional views down to the coast at **São Vicente**. There are a number of laurel species in the forest but the most dominant are Fetid Laurel or Til, Madeira Mahogany and Canary Island Laurel; the latter being the only one to host the fungi Laurobasidium lauri, which can be spotted along this route.

As the path starts a slight descent, we arrive at a T-junction and turn right. Twenty-five metres ahead we reach two finger posts (Wp.3 25M) - one pointing right (PR21 Caminho do Norte to Ribeira Grande), the other pointing left (PR22 to the ER228)

Laurobasidium lauri

We follow the route left for 100 metres to reach the road where there's another information panel and finger posts (Wp.4 35M). We cross over; a finger post directs us into the forest.

Fingerposts at Wp.4

Reaching a pretty stream and crossing over on a concrete slab, our route then makes a sharp U-turn (Wp.5 38M). We cross two more stream beds then continue ahead looking out for the path veering off to our right; there's a red and yellow field code sign here directing us. Note: this sign had been damaged on our second survey Jan 14 so if you find yourself going straight ahead at this point and end up at the stream on the left, go back and find the right hand path.

Along the forest path

We drop down a few stone and log steps before crossing a stony stream bed in a gully on our right; on the opposite bank we find another sign (Wp.6 50M).

The path follows the stream bed for a few metres before veering off right with the stream bed veering off left. The forest begins to thin out and the route becomes much clearer - we cross another stream on stepping-stones and find another field code sign to direct us.

Arriving at a T-junction (Wp.7), the field code sign doesn't appear to point in any direction, however our correct route turns left on the broader path soon crossing a wooden bridge over a stream (Wp.8 65M).

A little further along we reach a gulley which appears to cross our path, but getting closer we find our route turns left leading us back into the park.

A final field code sign appears alongside the road just before reaching the car park and the end of our trail back inside the park (Wp.1 75M).

31 ESTANQUINHOS to PICO RUIVO DO PAÚL CIRCULAR

Paúl da Serra (literally translating to 'swamp of the mountains') is a large plateau on the west of the island covering an area of around 22 km². This route, though quite short, is particularly rewarding as it takes in its highest point of **Pico Ruivo do Paúl** (1639 metres above sea level) providing magnificent views in all directions; unsurprisingly, the area is a magnet for walkers and nature lovers, attracting considerable numbers of visitors.

Our trail crosses a section of **Paúl da Serra** through low shrub land, mainly bracken, broom and gorse, the yellow blossoms magnificent when in bloom. You'll also find carpets of mountain thyme, violets, forget-me-nots and Canary buttercups.

Mountain thyme

In spring, loud croaking frogs will not fail to attract attention, having colonized the marshy areas close to the path. By taking a little detour they can be spotted as they plop into the water on our approach. Apparently these are Perez's Frog (Rana perezi), similar to Marsh Frogs and the only species found on the island. These were introduced to Madeira in the early 19th century.

Access by car or taxi:
Take the ER105 west from **Encumeada** for approximately 10 kms, passing the **Bica da Cana** picnic site on the right.

Around 2 kms ahead, turn right onto the ER208 signed 'Estanquinhos'. Alternatively, approach from the **Paúl da Serra** crossroads (1.6 km) Parking is available close to the junction.

Pico Ruivo do Paúl visible from the start

Starting at the road junction at **Estanquinhos** (Wp.1 0M), we follow a narrow *levada* as it heads northwest over open moorland. **Ruivo do Paúl** can be seen in the distance as it rises up from the bracken, its trig point on the flat summit clearly visible from the start. The path is quite stony in places, often making progress slow, but after passing beside a number of deciduous trees (Wp.2 10M) our route enters the coniferous woodland, soon arriving at a junction with a broad forest track on the right and the large barbeque area of **Fontes Ruivos** in a clearing straight ahead (Wp.3 20M).

Entering the woodland (Wp.2)

Fingerposts indicate two options; you can either keep following the *levada* to its source close to a water collection pit, then continue on a steep narrow track to the summit of **Ruivo do Paúl** or (our choice), turn right, making a slightly longer but gentler ascent to the summit.

Turning right at this junction, we follow the track through the woodland in the direction of the **Estanquinhos Forestry House**, fifteen minutes along arriving at a junction with another track, this one grassy and leading off left.

The ascent

The fingerpost here indicates the distance to **Pico Ruivo do Paúl** as 0.8km (Wp.4 35M). A short distance along we reach another junction with fingerposts (Wp.5 45M) and going left again, we begin the ascent to the summit.

Around fifty metres from the junction, the track splits, a broad right hand branch heading directly up to a viewing platform on the summit; this will be our return route but for now we continue straight ahead on a narrower path, making a much gentler gradient up the hillside.

Looking back, there are wonderful views of the central mountain range as well as the wind turbines across the plateau, the latter looking quite striking when the light is good.

On the summit

Keeping the trig point in view our route continues to follow the narrow path towards another fingerpost, soon meeting the alternative steeper path rising up from **Fontes Ruivos**. Joining this track we now turn right to make the final short ascent to the trig point (Wp.6 70M).

We are rewarded handsomely for our climb; we are 1639 metres above sea level and enjoy 360° views from this flattish summit. From the viewing platform on the northern escarpment there are magnificent views down the **São Vicente** valley with the full extent of **Paúl da Serra** around us and forested slopes sweeping away in all directions.

.. superb views ..

From here our route crosses to the eastern edge of the summit reaching another fingerpost (Wp.7 90M) which indicates our descent route back to **Estanquinhos** but first, a few metres beyond the sign, we find the second viewing platform, not only with superb views of the north coast but also views of the central massif.

Making a steep descent back to the junction at (Wp.5) and ignoring our inward route to this point, we now continue straight ahead on a narrow grassy path towards **Estanquinhos** and the ER208. Along this final section, the trail passes through another area of coniferous woodland before eventually reaching the forestry house (Wp.8 105M).

Turning right and descending the drive for 25 metres takes us to the ER208, the tarred access road leading up from the ER105. It's then a one kilometre stroll along this road, back to our starting point (Wp.1 120M).

Madeira Walks 1   113

32 FANAL TO CURRAL FALSO
(PR14 -LEVADA DOS CEDROS)

Levada dos Cedros

Fanal, on the north western edge of the **Paúl da Serra** plateau (1130 metres above sea level) is an area of immense beauty and tranquility where green grassy slopes, low shrubland and the heath and laurel forests converge. Popular for family picnics and barbeques at weekends and on public holidays, it's also an area for escaping and enjoying nature at its best.

Levada dos Cedros was built in the 17th century and excavated along the right hand bank of the **Ribeira da Janela** valley; it's said to be one of the oldest water channels on the island. The whole trail passes through well-conserved primitive forest, a wonderfully tranquil route with only bird sounds and trickling water to break the silence. Bathed in dappled sunlight, our path passes through lush vegetation, the canopy ensuring lots of shade even in the height of summer. Though some sections of the descent are steep, the pathway is well-laid with wooden steps to carry us down to the *levada* around 250 m below.

Access by hire car or taxi: follow the ER105 from **Encumeada** to the **Paúl da Serra** crossroads taking the ER209 north, signed 'Fanal & Ribeira da Janela' and continue for 8.1 kilometres to the start of the walk; this is signed on the left of the road just before the **Fanal Forestry Post**. If you prefer to cut out the ascent and descent and just enjoy the *levada*, you could start the walk at the end of the route at **Curral Falso**, which is 4km further along the ER209.

Leaving the information board (Wp.1 0M) we go down a few steps soon finding a stone cairn on our left. At first the trail descends through an area of heaths but soon transcends deep into the natural forest with its high canopy and dense vegetation.

As our descent gets steeper it becomes a series of steps which wind down to eventually cross a well-constructed rustic bridge (14M) before continuing down further flights of steps. These eventually become a steep zigzag from where we can hear the river as it tumbles down rocks at the source of the *levada*. We descend a little further, keeping an eye out to the right, where we now see the channel below us.

Soon we reach the *levada* at the bottom of the final descent, from where our route takes a short detour to the left to a strong flowing stream tumbling down beautiful waterfalls, which first feeds into the *levada* before continuing deeper into the valley below, to join the **Ribeira da Janela** (28M).

We retrace our steps to now following the *levada* downstream, the valley to our left getting deeper. However all precipitous sections are well protected with sturdy fencing and, other than short descents, the water channel maintains height as it clings to the forested valley side beside the rock face and the dense vegetation. A little further along we arrive at a stream at the head of a deep side valley (37M), from where the *levada* flows in a northerly direction soon arriving at a semi-circular paved area at the head of another valley.

.. a pretty viewing platform ..

Continuing, we next encounter a flight of steps to our left leading to a pretty viewing platform on a rocky outcrop, again well-constructed and protected (Wp.2 50M); we can take in fine views down the **Ribeira da Janela** valley, and also pick out the ER105 running along the ridge from **Fonte do Bispo** towards **Santa**.

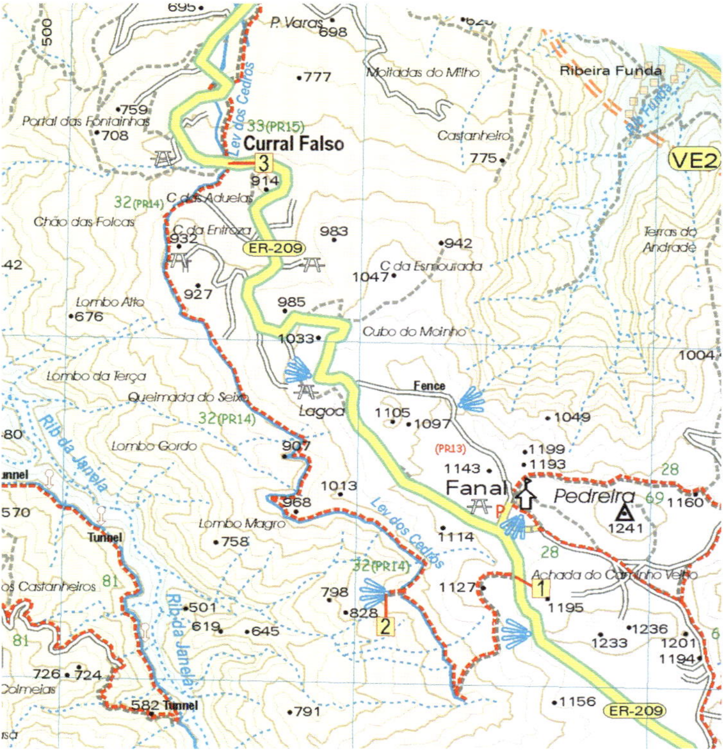

Following the *levada* once more, we round a side valley where another break in the forest provides us with a wonderful view of the distant forested slopes around **Galanho**.

Passing between sun and shade, the conditions along this trail are perfect for the many endemic species that thrive here, including the pink Madeira Orchid and bright yellow Giant Crowfoots, these attracting many butterflies, which flit in and out of the vegetation. The trail now crosses another bridge in a deep side valley (56M) and soon we arrive at a small stream tumbling down the black basalt rock into the *levada* (62M). Along these shady damper banks of the water channel, Liverworts, European Chain Fern and Madeira Hog Fennel also find the perfect habitat.

Surrounded by deep vegetation

Continuing, we eventually arrive in a semi-circular area at yet another small valley head, where stone seating has been provided and where we can rest and partake of our refreshments (92M).

The *laurisilva* is home to many of the island's resident bird population and sitting quietly here, the less shy species of finches, wagtails and blackbirds often make an appearance.

.. **the final rustic bridge** ..

Suitably refreshed we continue on, crossing the final rustic bridge over a gully (115M) then another stone seat behind the *levada* and, with not far to go, we soon pass a stone cairn, which appears on our right.

Immediately after this steps lead us down to the ER209 regional road (Wp.3 135M) at **Curral Falso**, the end of the trail; Walk 33 (PR15) starts on the opposite side of the road beside another information panel.

Curral Falso

33 CURRAL FALSO TO RIBEIRA DA JANELA (PR15 VEREDA DA RIBEIRA DA JANELA)

Ribeira da Janela, **Porto Moniz**'s smallest parish, takes its name from the largest of three rock stacks (**Ilhéus da Ribeira da Janela**) rising 57 metres out of the sea, the natural rock aperture in its centre resembling a *janela* or window. Predominantly a wine producing area, the village extends from the mouth of the river of the same name to an altitude of 400 metres, its houses scattered among traditional agricultural terraces of sweet potatoes, beans and maize and other crops. It also boasts Madeira's only campsite, close to the river mouth.

Ribeira da Janela 'Rockstack'

Our trail follows an ancient footpath used by local people to bring wood, essential to their daily lives, from the forested area above. It also connected the settlement with the south side of the island mainly **Calheta** and **Ponta do Sol** for trading and festivals.

Access by car or taxi:
Follow the ER209 from the **Paúl da Serra** crossroads signed 'Fanal & Ribeira da Janela', continuing for 12 km. The trail starts on the right of the road beside an information panel; it's possible to park beside the road.

For your return, you either need to follow the route back to the start or call a taxi from the end of the walk or from **Bar Achada** in **Ribeira da Janela**, to take you back to the starting point. A taxi will cost around €15. An alternative is to park near **Bar Achada** and then taxi to **Curral Falso**, then you'll be walking downhill back to your car.

Starting at the information board on the ER209 (Wp.1 0M), we pass a stone cairn on our right and descend on a logged stairway through the forest following **Levada dos Cedros**. A short distance ahead the channel and path separate although rushing water can still be heard. We reach the ER209 (Wp.2 15M) crossing over to pick up the path on the opposite side and a little way ahead we cross it once again.

The path is now wide and grassy, running parallel to the water channel, which at this point is audible though not visible. Descending wooden steps we rejoin the *levada* and get glimpses of the coast through the low tree line. Crossing the ER209 for the last time, we go right before turning left a few metres along to continue on the trail (Wp.3 30M).

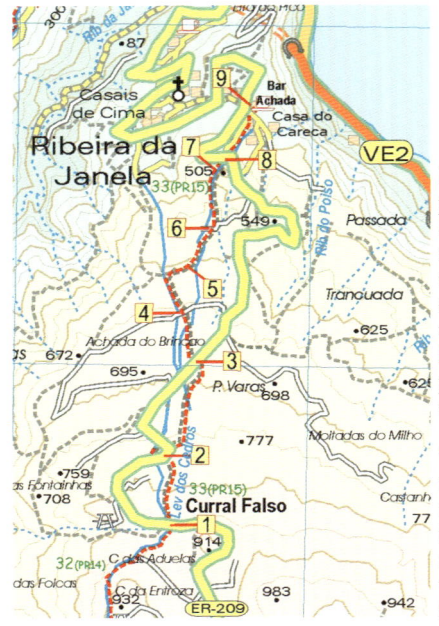

Descending from the road, the path narrows and soon the *levada* crosses our path so we step over it. Here the water channel goes off to our right, after which our route meets up with a broad forest track (Wp.4 35M) where we turn right, picking up the trail again a few metres along on the left.

The vegetation changes, with taller pines and eucalyptus sharing space with the heath trees. Stepping down another staircase, we reach a junction with a dry stonewall and rustic fencing.

Turning right, we follow the path for a few metres before it veers right again as we negotiate stone steps to reach a ladder stile on our left (Wp.5 50M).

Crossing over the stile and descending more wooden steps, we reach a junction with a broad earthen track which we follow right, ignoring a narrow path on the opposite side.

Rounding a bend to a point just before a stream crosses the track (Wp.6 65M), our route is signed off left, to descend another wooden stairway, the stream now coursing down on our right. The forest is again changing, this time to *laurisilva* as the heaths diminish.

One of the stepped descents

The path and steps here are very narrow but soon the forest opens up, giving us our first views of the village and the north coast. To our left are views of the southern slopes of the **Ribeira da Janela** valley, the line of the well-known walking route **Levada da Ribeira da Janela** (Walk 39) clearly visible along the forested slopes.

Along the next section we find the beautiful endemic Lily of the Valley trees (in flower around August time) as well as colourful colonies of Montbretia and Himalayan Ginger. As we emerge from the woodland, we have clear views of the nearby village.

Soon meeting another earthen track and a barn on our left, the track veers right, our route turning off left through the grassy banking beside the barn gate (Wp.7 80M).

The view from Bar Achada

Descending steeply and passing an A-framed farm building with a tin roof, we drop down the last few steps to reach the ER209 and the end of our trail (Wp.8 90M). There are now two choices; either to walk back to the starting point by the same route (allow 2 hours, 2.7 km, Ascent 440m), or to walk down to **Bar Achada** in **Ribeira da Janela** where you can arrange a taxi.

To continue down to the bar, we cross over the road taking a stepped descent between one or two houses to arrive again on the ER209. Crossing a second time, we follow a local pathway and turn right at a track junction to return to the road where a pedestrian crossing leads us to the bar (Wp.9 95M). The owner will call a taxi for you to return to the starting point at **Curral Falso**.

34 BICA DA CANA - PINÁCULO - CIRCULAR

Bica da Cana is a popular weekend picnic site for local people, when entire families spend the day barbecuing and relaxing in the woodland beside the forestry house. Our circular route heads firstly to the *miradouro* and trig point (1620m) with breathtaking views of the central massif, then drops into an area of natural forest along **Levada da Serra** lying on the north-eastern edge of the **Paúl da Serra** plateau. We take in a tranquil lunch spot at the foot of **Pináculo**, often referred to as Madeira's '**Sugar Loaf Mountain**' due to its elliptical shape, then return to the starting point along a section of Walk 72 Encumeada Circular (Madeira Walks Volume Two), high above the **São Vicente** valley.

On a recent survey we found the section after Wp.3 down to the *levada* to be quite overgrown with gorse; even though periodical maintenance is carried out, long trousers are recommended for this route.

There's plenty of botanical interest as the trail passes through areas of *laurisilva* and heath forest where endemic species thrive.

Sow thistles, Canary buttercups and Bilberry grow to huge proportions whilst Madeira orchids, wild geraniums, Mandon's chrysanthemum, mountain stock and stonecrops provide rich colour from spring through to autumn. Along the damper habitats of the *levada*, water dropwort, navelwort, liverworts and ferns flourish.

Madeira orchids

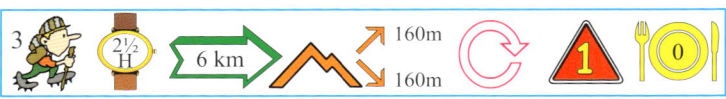

Access by car or taxi:
Take the VE4 north from **Ribeira Brava**, turning left on the ER105 for **Serra da Agua** and **Encumeada**. On reaching the summit, the road forks sharp left, continuing for around 8 km through the mountain pass; the forestry house and car park of **Bica da Cana** are located on the right of the road. From the north and west, approach from the **Paúl da Serra** crossroads taking the ER105 east for 4.5 km.

From the main gateway (Wp.1 0M) we follow a cobbled path veering left off the vehicle track to climb to the *miradouro* (Wp.2 12M) to take in spectacular views of Madeira's highest peaks; **Pico Ruivo** and **Pico do Areeiro** are in front of us, whilst the basalt outcrop of **Pináculo** is in sight lower down the valley.

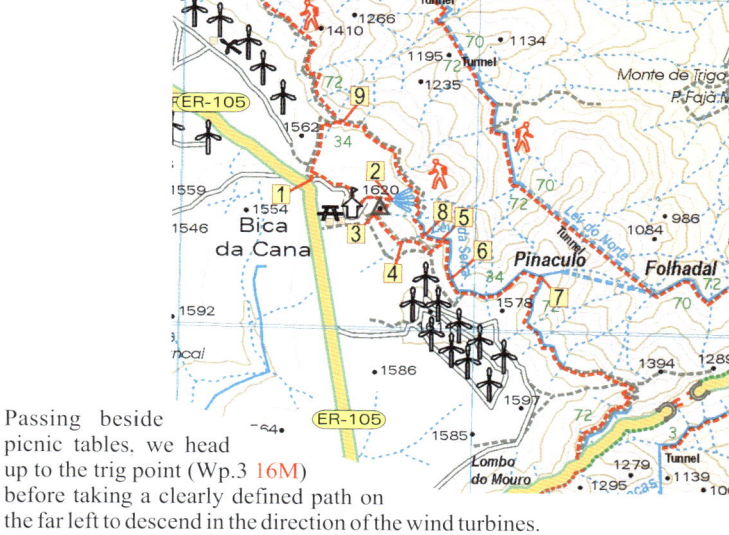

Passing beside picnic tables, we head up to the trig point (Wp.3 16M) before taking a clearly defined path on the far left to descend in the direction of the wind turbines.

We walk alongside a fence then reach a broken stile on our right (Wp.4 26M), immediately turning left and following a water channel for a few metres before crossing over it to continue our descent through the heather.

The descent to Pináculo (after Wp.3)

We pass a cairn before eventually emerging onto the shoulder of **Levada da Serra**, our route for the moment going right to follow the channel downstream (Wp.5 41M), although we return to this spot after visiting **Sugar Loaf**.

Heading towards **Pináculo** the aqueduct has been carved between the rock face and the mountain slopes of the **São Vicente** valley.

Now on a section of the official **PR17** route (our Walk 72) we pass a number of semi circular rock walls where water sprays into the channel, stunning when caught in the sunlight. The largest of these resembles a small amphitheatre; here a waterfall crashes down over the *levada*

.. a waterfall crashes down ..

Madeira Walks 1   121

(Wp.6 50M) so a raincoat might be a bonus at this point.

.. more views of Sugar Loaf ..

We push through lush yellow masses of flowering broom that often dominate the path. With more views of **Sugar Loaf** and the high peaks appearing through the vegetation, we eventually arrive at the base of **Pináculo** (Wp.7 62M), a lovely quiet place with stone seating, ideal for a stop or refreshments.

Walk 72 (Madeira Walks Volume Two) arrives at **Sugar Loaf** on a paved pathway coming up from the right of our path just beyond the seating area.

Back on our main route, we retrace our steps, passing the junction where we joined the *levada* and continuing along the channel shoulder in a westerly direction. We eventually reach a short flight of steps on our left leading up to a waterfall (Wp.8 102M).

Ignoring these, our route begins to undulate as we continue along the *levada* pathway for a further twenty minutes to reach a fingerpost directing us left back to **Bica da Cana** (Wp.9 127M). Walk 72 continues on to **Encumeada** from this point.

Our signed ascent to Bica da Cana

Leaving the *levada* at the fingerpost, we ascend a rocky stairway twisting up the hillside. Eventually the vegetation thins out as we continue to ascend, following the fence and tree line until arriving back on the ER105 at our starting point (Wp.1 138M).

35 LEVADA DAS 25 FONTES VIA CALHETA TUNNEL (PR6)

The **Rabaçal** valley on the western slopes of the **Paúl da Serra** plateau is one of the most beautiful locations on the island as well as one much frequented by walkers. **Levada das 25 Fontes** is the most well known and well walked trail in this area but if you seek peace and tranquility, we suggest visiting early in the morning or later in the day, to avoid the crowds. For this reason, and to make an easy out and back trail, we have chosen to start and end the route on the **Calheta** slopes where we can access the *levada* on a level pathway through the **Calheta** tunnel. This is around 800 m long but it's good underfoot and there's plenty of headroom. A good torch is essential.

It should be noted that sections of the *levada* shoulder are extremely narrow and precipitous and whilst these are very well protected with steel posts and fencing, care is needed along these sections. Bearing this in mind, it's a superb trail that can be enjoyed by most people.

Access by car or taxi:
Leave the ER222 in the centre of **Estrela da Calheta** following the ER211 for 5 km to reach the picnic site in **Lombo do Salão**. Alternatively approach from the ER105 **Paúl da Serra** road dropping down the ER211 towards **Calheta**. Park beside the shelter.

Access by bus:
Bus Nºs 80. 107 and 115 serve **Estrela da Calheta** but you will need to take a taxi from the centre to the start of the walk in **Lombo do Salão**. If you are using a taxi, be sure to arrange with the driver for your return journey.

Just above the picnic site (Wp.1 0M) we take a broad path heading off right into the forest signed '25 Fontes and Risco'.

Along the approach to the tunnel

We follow this along the valley side soon crossing a cattle grid to arrive at the pretty water-house at the head of the **Calheta** valley.

The water house near the Calheta slopes

Turning left beside the house, the tunnel stands a few metres ahead, its entrance a high archway, covered in ferns (Wp.2 15M).

It takes around 15 minutes to negotiate before reaching a platform above the valley with seating around it (Wp.3 30M).

On emerging, also look to the left for the pretty little shrine set into the rock.

The shrine as we emerge from the tunnel

Leaving the platform, water rushes down a chute on the right feeding into the channel before it flows into the tunnel, we follow the *levada* upstream, two minutes later arriving at steps on our right. These are signed 0.5 km to **Casa Rabaçal Forestry House**.

Our pathway is wide and comfortable; another few minutes along we pass through a large rock cutting then a path on our left descending into the valley (Wp.4 42M). This is the route to **Levada da Rocha Vermelha**, a channel flowing around 100 metres lower down the valley.

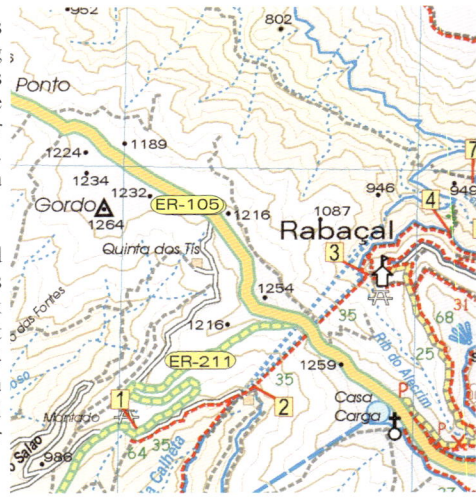

.. the shoulder narrows (after Wp.6)

It's only another few minutes before a paved stairway appears on our right (Wp.5 45M), this is the route up to **Levada do Risco** and also the route back to the Forestry Post and to the **Rabaçal** car park on the ER105; it's the traditional route for walkers visiting **25 Fontes**.

Continuing along the pleasant pathway we reach a flight of steps taking us down to a bridge over the **Ribeira Grande** (Wp.6 55M) and then ascending on the opposite side to a small water building above. From hereon the channel shoulder narrows and is fenced with steel posts and wire.

Around 400m beyond the **Ribeira Grande Bridge**, a stairway appears on our right; this is a new return route which has recently been constructed to improve safety to walkers and also to reduce the volume of traffic along the narrowest part of the *levada* which has caused serious erosion. Walkers are therefore asked to respect this diversion on their return to **Casa do Rabaçal**. The new route starts around 120 metres from the **25 Fontes**. The stairway is approximately 250m in length with an ascent and descent of 50m therefore reducing the original return journey by around one kilometre.

A path drops down to our left (Wp.7 83M), another route down to **Levada da Rocha Vermelha**, ignoring this we continue ahead soon arriving at an amphitheatre where the cliff face towers above us and the 25 natural springs cascade into a small lake at the base of the cliffs (Wp.8 90M).

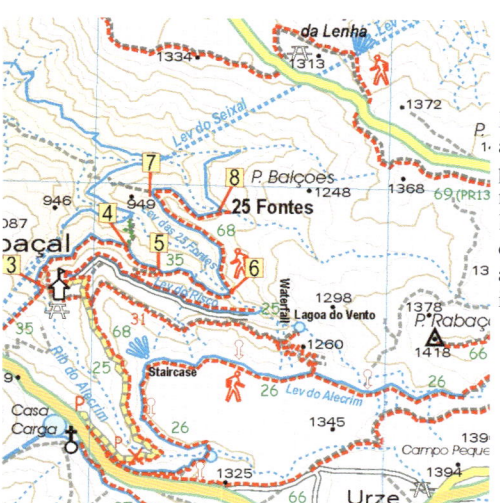

It's most unlikely that you'll be alone here; in fact you'll probably be surrounded by many happy walkers, eating lunch or enjoying a scramble over the large boulders in this area of lush green ferns and indigenous vegetation.

From here we now retrace our steps back to the starting point, again squeezing along the narrow pathways over the first section before enjoying the wide level pathway taking us back to the **Calheta** tunnel and onwards to our starting point at the picnic site on the ER211 (Wp.1 180M).

One of the 25 springs at the base of the cliffs

36 LEVADA DO MOINHO - PORTAS DA VILA - ACHADAS DA CRUZ

This trail, part of the official **PR7** route, follows a section of **Levada do Moinho** (The Mill Route) which opened to the public in 2008 and is as yet unknown to most visitors, so we may well have it all to ourselves. The full route of 10.3 kilometres runs from **Ribeira da Cruz**, close to the boundary of **Calheta** and **Porto Moniz**, to **Junqueira**, **Lamaceiros** where the well-known route of **Levada da Ribeira da Janela** begins (See Walk 39).

Our trail passes through one of the best preserved sections of the *laurisilva* on the north-west of the island, taking us along a spectacular walk with waterfalls, ravines, pools and sub-tropical vegetation, finally leading us to an ancient water mill at **Achadas da Cruz**.

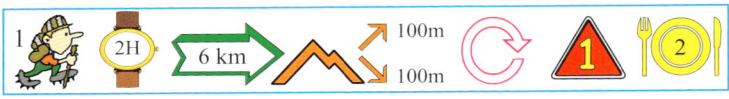

Access by car or taxi:
Take the ER105 over **Paúl da Serra** to reach the T-junction with the ER101 at **Portas da Vila**, **Santa** (a few kilometers above **Porto Moniz**). Park along the roadside next to the **Posto Florestal da Santa** forestry house.

Access by bus:
Rodoeste provide an infrequent and slow service on bus Nºs 80 and 107. These are unlikely to be suitable for anyone traveling from anywhere east of **Ribeira Brava**, though check with the bus company to ensure that the service fits with your needs.

The fingerpost at Wp.1

On the opposite side of the road from the forestry house a finger post, signed 'Ribeira da Cruz', directs us southwest (Wp.1 0M) where we climb a few steps and follow a narrow path to pick up the *levada*.

Turning right, our route passes a cairn before heading into the forest where it runs more or less parallel with the ER101.

We soon reach a water stairway (Wp.2 10M) before progressing deeper into this wonderful section of natural

The water stair at Wp.2

forest. We walk through dense subtropical vegetation, rocky cliffs and deep ravines where the vegetation is lush and waterfalls plunge into lovely pools formed behind the *levada*.

In places the irrigation channel is carved into the rock face, these damp and humid conditions supporting many species of lichens and mosses. Of particular interest is the abundance of liverwort covering the surrounding rocks and carpeting the pathway under our feet, while the European Chain Fern grows to huge proportions.

.. dense subtropical vegetation ..

This area is also the habitat of the Long-toed Pigeon (Columba Trocaz), one of only two Madeiran endemics - shy creatures who, if disturbed by our footsteps, will escape above the canopy giving us only a glimpse of fluttering wings.

At the head of the gorge

We reach the first of the two largest waterfalls, this one with a good surface underfoot and safety fencing, but expect to get wet after heavy rainfall unless you make a detour across the stream bed below the fall. The second waterfall is reached a few minutes later and is slightly more difficult, the crossing taking us over boulders and stones. There's less chance here of getting wet, but care is needed negotiating this section.

Shortly after leaving the waterfall, a path crosses the *levada* (Wp.3 25M). This emerges through a rustic gate on our left then drops down right to

Madeira Walks 1   127

reach the ER101, an alternative exit if the weather is bad.

The final gorge at **Ribeira do Tristão** is dark and damp with a waterfall and pool at the valley head. We negotiate this by crossing the weir and whilst the gorge is deep to our right, the pathway is protected. A few minutes ahead the natural forest diminishes (Wp.4 30M) and is abruptly taken over by an area of Eucalyptus and Pine, much of which has been cleared due to fire damage several years ago. The plus side of this is that we now get good views down to the coast.

Ascending a series of log steps (Wp.5 40M), we leave the *levada* for a short detour before rejoining it.

Montbretia

Along the next section our pathway is adorned with exotic flora; Passion flower from S. America, large yellow Ginger Lily from the Himalayas, Montbretia from S. Africa and European Fuchsia are all found here during the spring and summer months.

Although these large flowering species are a delight to the eye, they are unfortunately extremely invasive and so a threat to Madeira's endemic flora.

Heading back into more indigenous forest, we arrive at the water treatment building of **Reservatória Achadas da Cruz** across from which is a flight of steps on our right (Wp.6 55M), our route down to **Achadas da Cruz**. Ignoring the steps, we continue beside the *levada*, our path veering off left, soon crossing a narrow bridge. Passing through another gate, we then arrive at a derelict corn mill hidden in the trees. In the past, the *levada* was used to power the grinders of this historic little mill and it passed under the building through a small archway, which is still visible (Wp.7 62M).

The extended route to the source of the *levada* at **Ribeira da Cruz** and down to the start of the PR7 trail on the ER101 would take another 2 hours, but for our shortened circular walk we return to the steps at the water treatment building (Wp.6 70M). Here we have two choices; either to return the same way along the *levada* or to descend the steps to reach the ER101 (Wp.8 75M).

From the bottom of the stairway, we turn right following the road, soon passing a bar on our right. Following regional roads is not something I would normally recommend, but this reasonably quiet section of the ER101 is lined with agapanthus and hydrangea and passes through a stunning section of the natural forest; it's also a quicker route back to the starting point (Wp.1 120M).

37 SANTA - PORTO MONIZ

This short yet stunning walk takes in spectacular views of the north coast to be enjoyed by everyone who can manage the descent (walking pole recommended). Beginning close to the paroquial church of **Santa**, our route follows **Caminho do Pico**, an ancient cobbled trail zigzagging down the cliffs into the pretty town of **Porto Moniz**.

One of the most popular north coast tourist locations, **Porto Moniz** is probably best known for its outstanding natural seawater swimming pool, now expanded along the whole of the sea front.

In addition, the town has undergone substantial development, accommodating

São João Fort

Porto Moniz harbour

new hotels, restaurants and shops; it's also home to a *aquário* housed in the lovely old **São João Fort**, as well as a living science museum, the **Ciéncia Viva Centre**. Add to this the pretty harbour with its colourful fishing boats and the stunning coastal views; it's not surprising that visitors flock here throughout the year.

* circular with bus or taxi

Access by hire car or taxi:
Take the regional ER105 across **Paúl da Serra** to the junction with the ER 101 at **Portas da Vila**. Turning right, follow the signs for 'Porto Moniz' and continue for 1.8 kms to the village of **Santa**, parking close by the church. Alternatively, take your car into **Porto Moniz** and take the bus or a taxi to the start of the walk. A taxi costs around €10. There's a taxi stand in the centre of **Porto Moniz**.

Access by bus:
Rodoeste Bus Nºs 80 and 139 from **Funchal** and 150 from **Ribeira Brava** serve **Porto Moniz** and **Santa**; services from **Funchal** are extremely limited, therefore not recommended for this walking route.

However, if travelling by car to **Porto Moniz** then it is possible to find a limited service to take you to the start of the walk in **Santa** either at the beginning or the end. We suggest the 150 route currently leaving **Porto**

Moniz at 11.00 am arriving **Santa** church at 11.15 a.m. as the best option, but it's important to get an up to date bus timetable or check with the Tourist Office, before leaving.

Leaving the church in **Santa** (Wp.1 0M) we descend the ER101 road for a few metres before taking a tarred lane leading off to the left (Wp.2 3M), a few minutes later arriving at a crossroads (Wp.3 10M).

Going straight ahead to follow **Caminho do Pico**, we stroll through a gentle agricultural area before the road surface changes to a concrete lane and starts a very steep descent. Whilst it's quite tough on the knees along this stretch, we're rewarded with superb views of **Ilhéu Mole** islet with its pretty lighthouse as well as the harbour and the seawater pools of **Porto Moniz**. Eventually we arrive at a *miradouro* where the lane finally ends at a turning circle (Wp.4 33M).

To our right, steps lead us onto the ancient cobbled trail. After passing beside a house on the cliff top we begin snaking down the hillside, the gradient not as steep now, taking in dramatic views of the ER101 with its hairpin bends and patchwork of tiny fields while to the south, *laurisilva* forested slopes complete this picturesque scene.

Corn Poppies alongside our route

The vegetation along the descent is typical of the rugged north-western cliffs, supporting Giant Reeds, Houseleeks and Globe Flowers with Corn Poppies, Sea-Stocks and Sow Thistles providing stunning contrast.

Rock Navelwort (Umbilicus rupestris), a species mostly confined to the *laurisilva*, can also be spotted growing in the clefts of rocks and walls along this route, its tall dense flowers appearing in early summer.

Soon the path drops into denser vegetation in the valley bottom before crossing a small stream and heading towards the outskirts of the old town. Remnants of past cultivation remain, with Mango, Fig and Loquat trees flanking the route and a narrow *levada* flowing on our right. Eventually the cobbled track comes to an end at a junction with a newly tarred road leading from the ER101.

Our route goes left, though a short detour to the right will bring us to **Snack Bar A Latada** (Wp.5 63M), across from which is a wonderful *miradouro* providing fantastic view of the whole of the town and coastline.

Porto Moniz as seen from the old town

Back on our route, we descend the tarred road lined with new and older properties and small vineyards and soon, after a sharp right hand bend, we leave the tarred road on a steep concrete lane which takes us into a small square.

Approaching Nossa Sra. da Concéicão church

Following the sign for 'Caminho Pedro Mole' (Wp.6 68M), we pass along a quaint cobbled alleyway running between charming cottages with lovely gardens, where Wisteria hangs over the garden walls, the spire of **Porto Moniz** church dominating the vista ahead.

This attractive 17th century church built by Francisco Moniz is dedicated to Nossa Sra. da Concéicão. As we approach the building, a newly-paved pathway leads us between the church and a charming well and into the town's municipal square (Wp.7 71M).

Taking the ER101 regional road on our final section, we descend into the town, soon turning left following a sign for 'Piscinas' (swimming pools) (Wp.8 80M) and as we arrive at a junction in front of the post office (Wp.9 87M) our route turns right leading us to the sea front with its selection of bars, restaurants and gift shops (Wp.10 90M).

If you left your car at Santa, take a taxi or bus back to the start. The bus stops are situated close to the roundabout above the harbour, and in the Municipal Square, Wp.7). An alternative for the more energetic of course, is to retrace your steps back along **Caminho do Pico** to the starting point at **Santa** church.

38 LEVADA NOVA - FAJÃ DA OVELHA to PONTA DO PARGO

Since the opening of the VE3, the west of the island has become an extremely popular destination for walkers; eventually, this highway will reach **Ponta do Pargo**. Our walk follows a section of **Levada Nova**, which in total flows 50 km along the south west coast from its source

.. lovely views of the coastline ..

O Farol

above **Ponta do Sol** to its termination in **Cabo**.

The channel, at a height of 640m, crosses open hillsides with lovely views of the coastline along this western section. We negotiate a number of valley heads and dip in and out of woodland and head through agricultural settlements on this tranquil and safe trail. It's an ideal walk for breaking down into shorter sections as it crosses over the ER101 in three places, noted in our text. There's also an optional extension at the end of the trail to include a circular route to the sea cliffs.

Ponta do Pargo, at the far western point of the island, boasts the manned lighthouse of **O Farol** sitting on the sea cliffs with a *miradouro* and **Casa de Chá** close by. It's also an important area for Madeiran birds, where many terrestrial species as well as seabirds, can be spotted.

Access by hire car or taxi:
Take the VE3 west towards **Prazeres** village, continuing on the ER101 before turning left onto the ER223 signed 'Paúl do Mar'. **Levada Nova** crosses over the road 100m below the junction.

Access by bus:
Rodoeste bus routes N°80, 107 & 142 operate between **Funchal**, **Ribeira Brava** and **Ponta do Pargo**, though routes are slow and infrequent; they are adequate, though for the return from the end of the walk back to your car. Alternatively, use a taxi to return.

Leaving the ER223 (Wp.1 0M) we head off right along the channel shoulder, our path swinging right and passing through a stand of pines before continuing beside agricultural plots where superb views of the coast open up.

In spring and summer the footpath is flanked with wild flowers; honeysuckle, Madeira crane's-bill, sweet violets, calla lilies and morning glory can be found. Also not to be missed is the frequent appearance of damsel flies, Monarch butterflies (Danaus plexippus) and the Clouded Yellow (Colias crocea) flitting between the plants. In the cooler weather, the Migratory Locust (Locusta migratoria) can also be seen. Along most of the trail the *levada* is flanked by bracken, bramble and gorse; we are soon aware of Madeira Wall Lizards scurrying into the undergrowth.

Arriving at the hamlet of **São Lourenço** (Wp.2 15M), we cross over a narrow lane dotted with A-framed barns to pick up the channel on the opposite side, heading in a northerly direction and around

Colina da Fajã hotel

Madeiran Wall Lizard

a valley head. We arrive in **Sitio de São João** beside the pretty **Colina da Fajã** hotel (Wp.3 30M), a strikingly designed building with a wonderful olive tree in the front garden. At this point the *levada* is culverted so we pick it up again around 15 metres ahead on the left of the concrete lane. Two minutes after crossing another narrow lane beside a pretty pink house, we head out along the open hillside, at this elevation enjoying increasingly lovely views down to the sea.

The channel soon turns right and below us on our left, is **Rua das Eirinhas**, the second main road leading into **Fajã**. A few minutes later we reach the ER101 regional road, completing the first section of the trail (Wp.4 45M).

Crossing over, our path is now elevated above the road as it follows the contours. There's evidence of the new highway development, where tunnel entrances have appeared on either side of the valley. Continuing, we head into the **Ribeira dos Marinheiros** valley, a pretty section with rocky walls, rivulets and lush vegetation. Soon we hear the sound of rushing water as the river below us cascades over its stony bed. At the valley head, we cross on a stepped bridge (Wp.5 55M) with waterfalls and pools to our right, then head out of the valley back towards the regional road.

There's a short section to follow where there are a few unprotected drops; though these are minor and there's lots of vegetation, nevertheless care needs to be taken here. Another few minutes walking and we again cross the ER101 at a picnic and barbecue site (Wp.6 65M), picking up the channel around 10 metres ahead. Our route leads us through the settlement of **Lombo dos Marinheiros**, crossing cultivated fields, agricultural terraces and orchards

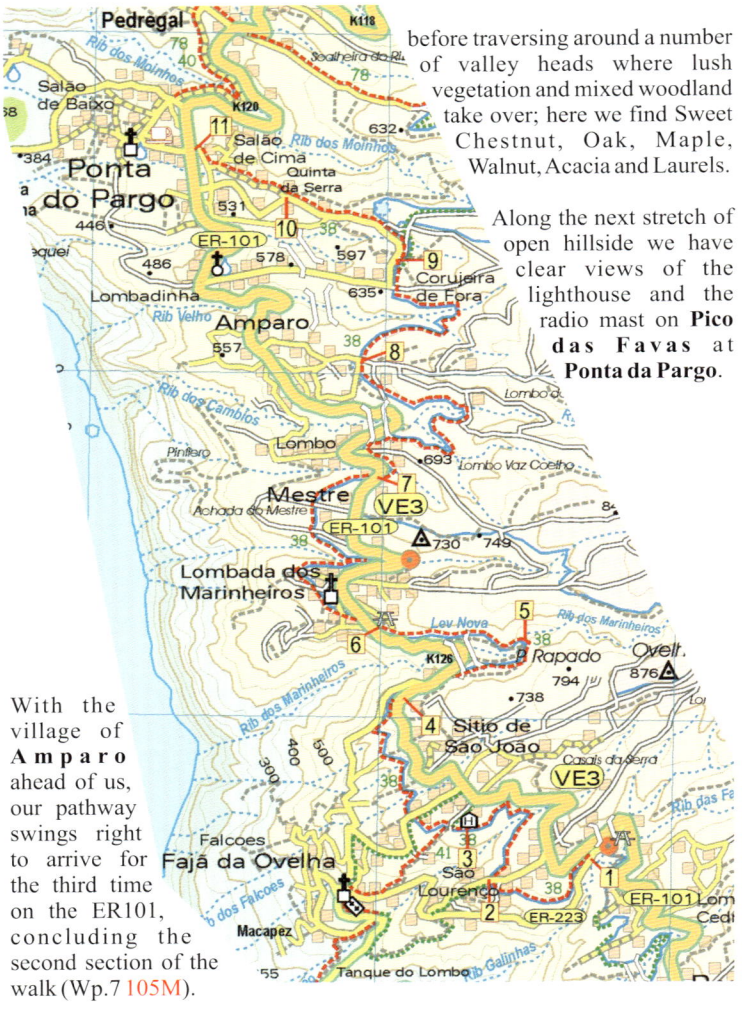

before traversing around a number of valley heads where lush vegetation and mixed woodland take over; here we find Sweet Chestnut, Oak, Maple, Walnut, Acacia and Laurels.

Along the next stretch of open hillside we have clear views of the lighthouse and the radio mast on **Pico das Favas** at **Ponta da Pargo**.

With the village of **Amparo** ahead of us, our pathway swings right to arrive for the third time on the ER101, concluding the second section of the walk (Wp.7 105M).

Crossing over the road, the channel loops behind a newly created picnic area where picnic tables, barbecue facilities and toilets can be found. Following the *levada* from the picnic site, our route heads through a small hamlet with apple orchards and orange groves. The trail leads into an agricultural area before arriving at a valley head amongst abundant eucalyptus where we cross a pretty river by means of a weir. We head out of the valley through a stand of pines before the sound of rushing water heralds our arrival at a second valley head; after crossing a track, we reach a beautiful spot with another river tumbling over waterfalls. We climb a few steps to cross over the weir before descending to the opposite bank.

Approaching another farming community, again with lots of A-framed barns, we cross a road above **Amparo** (Wp.8 155M). After another few minutes walking, as more houses appear, our path runs parallel with a tarred road. A

.. orange groves ..

few metres ahead, we arrive at a concrete driveway and leave the *levada* to drop onto the road (Wp.9 170M). (Note: The irrigation channel continues from here for another 8 kms to its end in **Cabo**, a parish of **Ponta do Pargo**. This takes over 2 hours to walk with a descent of 180 m to the chapel and headland (see Walk 78). Turning right along the road, we head down towards **Ponta do Pargo**. Around 700 metres ahead, we take a right fork signed 'Rua Salão de Cima' (Wp.10). On reaching a *fonte* we follow the road right and then left, to end in the village centre (Wp.11 190M), a total of 1.2kms from the *levada* with a descent of 150m; a taxi costs around €10-€15 (see Appendix for phone numbers); the bus stop is close to the junction on the ER101.

A Madeiran woman tends her crops

Extension

An extension can be added to the end of our walk, visiting **O Farol**, the *miradouro* and **Casa de Chá** restaurant, both situated on the headland below the village. The landscape around the lighthouse is wild, open grassland, the coastline is magnificent and in spring the wild flowers are a delight. Allow around one hour for this 4km extension with an additional descent and ascent of 170m.

Casa de Chá

Leave the ER101 on the opposite side of the road dropping down to the church then continue to descent between the houses. A road comes in from the right, this is part of a new road network developed for the proposed golf course, plans for which appear to have been suspended or abandoned. Ignoring this road we continue to the end of the lane to reach a *miradouro* and **Casa de Chá** (is open daily except Mondays and throughout February). From here a path crosses the top of the cliffs to connect with the lighthouse where a new road climbs up to the village passing **Pico das Favas** to arrive back on the ER101.

39 LEVADA DA RIBEIRA DA JANELA - LAMACEIROS

The **Ribeira da Janela** gorge which runs from **Rabaçal** down to the north coast is one of the most extensive areas of unspoiled landscape on the island. The *levada* of the same name follows its contours for fifteen kilometres, providing unforgettable views almost every step of the way.

Lamaceiros is the most popular access point, our trail following a six kilometre stretch initially along a well-manicured path lined with agapanthus and hydrangea, before heading deeper into the valley and the natural forest. We negotiate two tunnels en-route (a torch is needed) separated by a spectacular gorge and waterfall. Our final destination is an old *levada* house, an ideal spot for a picnic with magnificent views from the terrace and the company of tame chaffinches eager for titbits.

The attractively landscaped area around the start at **Lamaceiros** water house also offers barbeque buildings, toilets and play areas as well as an adjacent bar/restaurant.

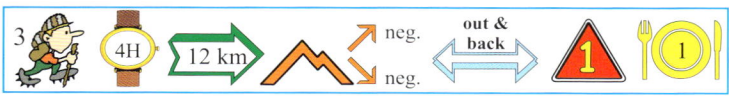

Access by car or taxi:
Leave **Porto Moniz** on the ER101 for the zigzag climb up the escarpment to reach a roundabout. Going left, a new, well-signed section of road continues through the village to the **Lamaceiros** water house. From easterly or southerly areas follow the ER105 over **Paúl da Serra,** turning right onto the ER101. **Lamaceiros** and the *levada* are signed off right a short distance below the junction.

Access by bus:
Rodoeste buses N° 80 (via south-west coast) and 139 (via **São Vicente**) travel between **Funchal** and **Porto Moniz**. Bus N°150 runs from **Ribeira Brava** to **Porto Moniz** and **Santa**. All are slow and infrequent and you will need to take a taxi for the final section up to **Lamaceiros**.

We start our walk by picking up the channel beside the water tanks, following it right on a grassy path alongside the rustic fencing.

Crossing over a tarred road, our route is signed (Wp.1 2M) as it heads in and out of the woodland beside flower-filled borders along the well-constructed channel, the pathway wide and good underfoot.

The sign at Wp.1

Along the channel shoulder

Six minutes later, we pass the first of three picnic areas strategically placed to take in the magnificent views along this route. We reach the second picnic site a few minutes later (Wp.2 18M) and look down the valley to the riverbed and the **Janela** rock on the coastline.

Oxalis purpurea

The natural forest takes over, becoming dark and humid and soon we pass beside a large water run-off (Wp.3 46M). Purple flowering sorrel (Oxalis purpurea) adorns our route as we pass into the denser forest contouring around numerous valley heads.

Occasionally small waterfalls spray down the sheer rock walls and here many species of fern and lichens thrive.

Rounding a rocky valley head, we arrive at the entrance to the

Madeira Walks 1 137

.. we emerge from the tunnel ..

first tunnel (86M), just under 200m long and taking around nine minutes to walk through; the path is quite wet and muddy in places, but it's reasonably good underfoot. Don't forget your torch!

We emerge from the tunnel above a deep gorge where a spectacular waterfall cascades over the *levada* (95M). It's such a beautiful spot and we don't even need to get wet as an amazing tin roof protects us from the flow; there's also safety rustic fencing around the arc of the gorge.

A few metres beyond the waterfall, the *levada* enters the second tunnel (100M); this is quite short but curves in the middle, the end only visible from the halfway point.

.. a spectacular waterfall ..

A few metres after exiting, the channel is covered with concrete slabs and the *levada* cut against the rock walls; it's quite precipitous but hand rails are provided for security.

Around fifteen minutes after the tunnel we arrive at an old *levada* water house (120M), a pleasant spot for a rest and to take in the views.

Emerging from the second tunnel

We've reached the end of the trail and we return by the same route, enjoying the different perspectives on the homeward journey. Once back at the tarred road at **Lamaceiros** (Wp.1 240M) we turn left, passing the car park on our right, to reach the bar/restaurant for some welcome refreshment.

If you require a taxi back to Porto Moniz, ask in the bar or refer to Appendix A for taxi telephone numbers. A taxi will cost around €10.

Alternatively, those wishing to walk back to the town can take the **Lamaceiros** road west as far as **Santa** church on the ER101, picking up Walk 37 to descend **Caminho do Pico** on the scenic route into the centre of **Porto Moniz**. (Allow 2 hours, 8kms, descent 460m).

40 PONTA DO PARGO to CABO

This walk along country lanes makes a lovely alternative to *levada* and mountain trails and here one can stride out, take in the views and soak up the atmosphere of this tranquil area in the west of the island. (See Walk 38 for further information on **Ponta do Pargo**.) Our undulating trail passes through a number of hamlets before arriving at **Cabo**, perhaps the prettiest headland on the island with its striking white chapel and grassy promontory to the cliff edge. There are also two detours along the route, one to a trig point on the cliffs with more splendid views along the coastline, another to an old school house in **Lombo Quinedo** where a tiny shrine sits snugly in an enormous eucalyptus tree.

Access by hire car or taxi:
Follow the VE3 and ER101 to **Ponta do Pargo** taking the second left signed 'Pico das Favas'. A few metres ahead you reach a junction with the village road and a sign post on the right for **Caminho Velha**. This is our route to **Cabo**. Park around this junction

Access by bus:
Rodoeste's Nºs 80, 107 & 142 provide an infrequent service between **Funchal**, **Ribeira Brava** and **Ponta do Pargo**; it's essential to arm yourself with a timetable before setting out.

From our start at the village junction (Wp.1 0M) we follow **Caminho do Velha**, a concrete lane descending off to the right running almost parallel to the ER101. The road dips into the valley, climbing on its opposite side to reach **Pedregal**, a pretty hamlet of traditional buildings with well tended gardens offering magnificent displays of Wisteria and Jasmine in spring.

We pass a drinking well on our right (Wp.2 20M) - the first of many along this route - then a junction with a road off right which we ignore, continuing along the country lane to reach a cross roads in the hamlet of **Serrado** where we go straight ahead, passing another well on our right (Wp.3 30M). The traditional Portuguese houses here are noteworthy; many are derelict and abandoned, but displaying elegant and ornate carvings around the doors and windows. Leaving this hamlet and following **Caminho do Velha**, the road now bends right and descends, passing yet another drinking fountain on the right (Wp.4 36M).

.. elegant, ornate carvings ..

A few minutes ahead we cross a bridge over **Ribeira da Vaca** (river of the cows), aptly named in this farming area (Wp.5 41M). From the river, our route then ascends into **Lombo Quinedo**. A large palm tree announces the start of the hamlet; to the left is the old derelict schoolhouse and a copse of large date palms. We detour left on **Impasso do Pico** beside an impressive new house (Wp.6 46M) taking us to a pretty little shrine set into the trunk of an enormous eucalyptus tree in front of the old building.

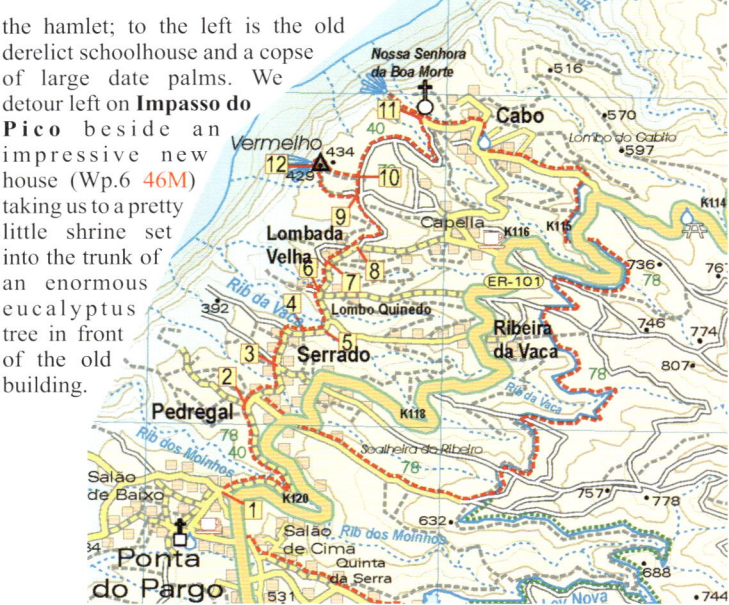

A cow tethered alongside the route

Turning back onto **Caminho do Velha**, our route leaves **Lombo Quinedo**, making another short ascent to the next hamlet of **Lombada Velha**, another drinking well appearing on our right (Wp.7 52M).

The old schoolhouse

As the lane ascends through the village, look out for a left turn onto **Caminho da Cruz**, signed 'Capela' (Wp.8 60M), a short tarred road which

Capela Nossa Senhora do Boa Morte

becomes a wide earthen track after the second house. The track leaves the village behind and contours around a small valley of low shrub land. We reach a cross road of earthen tracks (Wp.9 69M); left will be our exit route from the trig point at **Vermelho**, which we'll take on our return journey, but for now we continue in the direction of **Cabo**. Passing a second track off to the left (Wp.10 72M), our detour route to the trig point, we continue ahead for a few metres and on approaching a sparse woodland of eucalyptus and pine, we take in our first view of **Capela Nossa Senhora do Boa Morte**, the solitary white chapel at **Cabo**. There are two routes to it; one drops into the valley just before the track bends right; our

The headland at Cabo

.. wonderful views ..

route maintains height and continues around the valley head before arriving at the car park beside the chapel (Wp.11 90M), a beautiful spot above the headland. The original early 17th century chapel, now rebuilt, retains many original features, the architectural style typical Portuguese.

It's well worth a visit to see the Baroque altar and lovely furnishings (check at the church in **Ponta do Pargo** for opening times). From the chapel, a narrow concrete path can be seen heading across the low grassy promontory leading to a *miradouro* on the cliff edge allowing fine views along the coastline and an ideal place for a picnic (allow 20 mins return for this extension).

Our return from **Cabo** back to the starting point is by the same route, but around twelve minutes from the chapel, back at (Wp.10), we turn right to make a short detour to the trig point of **Vermelho**. The path drops down for a short distance, reaching a T-junction with a track coming down from the left. Here we turn right and follow a short incline to the cliff edge (Wp.12 115M) - the views are stunning. A few metres to the left we can look east, back to the **Ponta do Pargo** lighthouse, but care is needed here as there is no protective fencing along these cliffs. From the cliff edge a number of paths rejoin the track at the T-Junction, our route now continuing straight ahead to return to our main track (Wp.9 125M). Going right, we return to the hamlet of **Lombada Velha** before continuing the final stretch of our journey via **Serrado** and **Pedregal** back to the start (Wp.1 195M).

Extension: (Allow 1 hour return)
Once back in **Ponta do Pargo** you can extend this route by visiting the lighthouse and *miradouro* at **Casa de Chá**. Turning right at the junction (Wp.1) descend the road to reach the new road for the intended golf complex and continue to descend to the lighthouse **O Farol**, open daily and providing information not only of this location but of other lighthouses around the archipelago. From here there's a path across the cliff tops to **Casa da Chá** and the *miradouro*. The teashop opens daily throughout the year (not Mondays, closed February.) Return along the road beside the tea house leading up to the church and village centre.

41 FAJÃ DA OVELHA to PAÚL DO MAR

There was a time before the creation of the regional roads when **Paúl do Mar** was only accessible by boat or along the rugged cliff paths linking the village to trade and amenities in other settlements. We follow one of these ancient cobbled pathways, except for short sections where the route has been obliterated by development where we follow a short stretch of road to link the pathway in **Mazapez**. Starting at an elevation of 600m and dropping to sea level, this trail has a reasonably good descent, except for one or two damaged sections where care is needed. Otherwise, the zigzag route eases the overall gradient significantly.

Paúl do Mar harbour

The views from the cliffs are wonderful; once down, you'll feel the buzz of this lovely traditional fishing village nestled in its stunning position beneath the cliffs. There are a number of bars and restaurants

The bronze statue

and a wander through the enchanting narrow streets leading to the harbour is a must. Also impressive is the bronze statue erected on a rocks looking out to sea, erected as a tribute to fishermen past and present.

Access by car or taxi:
Take the VE3 towards **Fajã da Ovelha**, continuing on the ER101 before turning left onto the ER223 signed 'Paúl do Mar'; **Levada Nova** crosses over the road 100m below the junction. Hire car users should note that there is almost no bus service suitable for return to the start of the routs, therefore we recommend taking a taxi back to the start. There's a taxi located close to the harbour beside **Bar de Pescadores**; the fare will be in the region of 12 - 14€.

Access by bus:
Rodoeste provide a limited service on route Nºs 80, 107 and 142 between **Funchal**, **Ribeira Brava** and **Ponta do Pargo**. Alight at the junction of the ER101 and ER229. Return from **Paúl do Mar** on bus Nº80 (at 12.00 noon daily or 2.00pm weekdays only) or taxi back to **Calheta** to connect with bus services. It is important to pick up bus timetables before setting out.

The walk starts on the ER223 where the *levada* crosses the road. We follow it west for 30 minutes to reach the **Colina da Fajã Hotel** in **Sitio de São João**. Up to this point, we are walking the same route as Walk 38, waypoints 1-3. Once at this charming hotel and hamlet, we leave the *levada* to take a concrete drive on the left of the courtyard, signed 'Vereda da Soalheita'. Dropping down steps facing an old cottage, the route veers right as our descent on the ancient cobbled trail to **Paúl do Mar** begins.

Passiflora actinia

Soon crossing a driveway and passing a barn on our left, we reach a thicket of trees on our right; as our path becomes steeper and uneven, the church and steeple come into view. Meeting a T-junction of paths with the area in front fenced, we turn right and then immediately left, to drop down beside the fenced land.

A few metres ahead, look out for the wonderful scented Passiflora actinia as we descend a quaint narrow pathway between houses and gardens to arrive again on the ER223 (Wp.4 48M). Crossing the road, we head towards the church of **Fajã**, a lovely building of Moorish influence.

On reaching the main gates, we descend the steps turning right behind the church, to reach the ER223 where we then go left (Wp.5 50M). Our trail follows the road for a short distance before taking a right turn just beyond a bend, signed 'Rua Dr. Mário Correia Sardinha' (Wp.6 55M). We reach the area of **Macapez** where we pick up a path on the left with a ceramic sign indicating 'Antigo Fio da Fajã da Ovelha' (Wp.7 70M), approximately 800m in total from the church. Following the cobbled path, we descend to a stone bridge over the **Ribeira São João** and climb the opposite bank where the path peaks on the cliff tops. **Paúl do Mar** is now in view and we begin our main descent. Passing between two derelict cottages, we arrive at the **Antigo Fio**, a cable lift used to transport

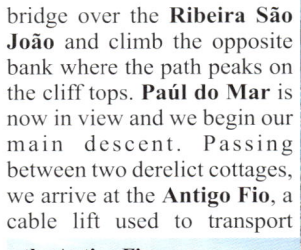
Looking down on Paúl do Mar

the Antigo Fio

produce between **Paúl** and **Fajã**, sitting on a platform on the cliff tops. Remnants of the old cable lift, wheel and buildings still remain in this attractive area surrounded by rustic fencing, which is also a superb lookout point (Wp.8 80M).

Another interesting feature of this area is the dominance of Agave Americana or Century Plant (referring to the long time the plant takes to flower). This South American tropical species, introduced to Europe in the 17th century, is now widely cultivated. With its large basal rosette of fibrous blue-green sword shaped leaves (as shown in our photo, above) and yellow flowers which grow into tall trees, it's quite remarkable.

From here on, our route becomes quite steep as it zigzags down the cliffs, passing beside ochre coloured volcanic rock along much of its descent. We reach a cave on our left (Wp.9 90M) and the further we drop, views of the hairpin bends and tunnels carved through rock of one of the island's most spectacular roads appear dramatically. Vegetation along the cliffs includes Globularia, Prickly Pear, Pride of Madeira and Houseleeks; also look out for the rare wild olive trees, a Madeiran endemic that grows on the precarious slopes of these cliffs.

Descending the cobbled path

Approaching sea level, the vegetation changes; bananas and other crops appear as the trail passes through the hamlet of **Ribeira das Galinhas**. A few metres after crossing the bridge (Wp.10 105M) we arrive on **Avenida dos Pescadores Paúlenses**, the **Paúl do Mar** promenade. Soon passing **Bar da Pedra** and **Maktub Bar** on our left - convivial places to stop for a drink (Wp.11 110M) - we head along the sea front to the area of **Igreja**. As the road bends left (Wp.12 125M), our route continues straight ahead through charming narrow streets, to arrive at the harbour (Wp.13 135M).

GLOSSARY

In addition to Portuguese words used in the text, we include other frequently encountered local words.

A
- *achada* — plateau
- *aeroporto* — airport
- *água* — water
- *alto* — high
- *autocarro* — bus

B
- *baía* — bay
- *baixo* — low
- *bica* — spring
- *boca* — mountain pass

C
- *caldeirão* — cauldron shaped crater or rock basin
- *caminho* — path, country road
- *campo* — field, plain
- *caniço* — reed
- *centro de saúde* — medical centre
- *choupana* — hut, cottage
- *cima* — above
- *correios* — post office
- *cova* — cavern
- *cruz* — cross
- *curral* — animal pen

E
- *estrada* — road

F
- *faial* — beech trees
- *fonte* — spring
- *furado* — levada tunnel

G
- *gaviota* — gull

I
- *ilhéu* — island

J
- *jardim* — garden

L
- *lago/lagoa* — lake, pool
- *lamaceiros* — marsh land
- *levada* — water channel
- *lombada* — mountain ridge

M
- *mar* — sea
- *mercado* — market
- *miradouro* — viewing point
- *monte* — mountain

P
- *palheiro* — thatched cottage or animal shelter
- *palmeira* — palm
- *paragem* — bus stop
- *pastelaria* — cake shop
- *paúl* — marshland
- *penha* — cliff, ridge
- *pico* — peak (mountain)
- *poço* — well
- *poio* — agricultural terrace
- *pomar* — orchard
- *ponte* — bridge
- *porto* — port
- *posto florestal* — forest house
- *pousada* — government run hotel

Q
- *quebrada* — steep slope, ravine
- *quinta* — farm house, country manor

R
- *ribeira* — river
- *risco* — danger

S
- *serra* — mountain range
- *sol* — sun

T
- *teleférico* — cable car
- *torre* — tower

V
- *vale* — valley

APPENDIX A
USEFUL INFORMATION

TAXIS

Taxis are often necessary for getting around both for sightseeing and for accessing walking trails. Phone numbers for taxis around the island are shown in the box below and whilst these were found to be current at the time of publication, some may change over time.

There are also two cooperative taxi services:-
Taxi Madeira - island wide service   912000625   www.taximadeira.com
Madeira Island Taxis - Funchal   291 764 476   www.madeira-island-taxis.com

The dial code for Madeira from overseas is +351

The main **taxi stands in Funchal** are located at:-

- Estrada Monumental and Forum Shopping in the Lido area
- Avenida Arriaga next to Municipal Gardens
- Largo dos Varadouros beside the Town Gate off Avenida do Mar
- Old Town off Rua do Carlos
- Madeira Shopping Centre
- Dolca Vita Shopping Centre
- Funchal Hospital - Avenida Luis de Camões

Calheta	919695861 966038547	Square	917242216 968778722
Estrela da Calheta	966038547	Ponta do Sol	291 972110
Prazeres	919695861	Portela	917842473
Cabo Girão	965010106	Paúl do Mar	962694875
Camacha	291 922185	Porto Cruz	291 572416 291 562411
Câmara de Lobos	291 942700 291 942407	Porto Moniz/	
Estreito de Câmara de Lobos	965010106	Lamaceiros	966045524 962583641 912000625
Caniçal	291 961989 917323630		926490313
Caniço	291 932156 291 933022	Ponta do Pargo/	
Canhas	291 972470 917323630 919514041	Amparo/Cabo Ribeira Brava	291 882165 968057129 291 952349 291 952606
Faial	291 572416		966045604
Fontes & Jardim da Serra	966033815 291 222000	Ribeira da Janela	966033815 96258364 912000625 926490313
Funchal:	910 799 756 291 764476 968778722 (24 hr)	Santa Cruz Santana	291 524888 969716933 291 572540 965013922 926612035
Machico	917842473 291 962480 291962220 291963666	Santo da Serra	917842473 917886342 96202821
Maroços & Ribeira Seca	917840983	São Vicente	291 842238
Monte / Babosas			

USEFUL PHONE NUMBERS

Emergencies	112	Motorway Assistance (VE)	800 20 30 40
Airport	291 520 888	Coastguard	291 700 112
Police	291 208 200	Assistance at Sea	291 230 112
Motorway Assistance(V1)	800 290 290	Red Cross (Cruz Vermelha)	291 741 115

TOURIST INFORMATION

The Tourist Offices listed below are the 'official' Madeira Tourist Authority offices:-

Main Tourist Office, **Funchal** 291 211 900/902
Direcção Regional do Turismo info@madeiratourism.org
Avenida Arriaga No 18, 9004-519 **Funchal** www.madeiratourism.org

Tourist Office, **Monumental Lido** 291 775254
C.C. Monumental Lido, Estrada Monumental, 284, 9000-100 **Funchal**
Mon to Fri 9.00 a.m. - 8.00 p.m. Sat 9.00 a.m. - 2.00 p.m.

Tourist Office at **Airport**, Santa Catarina de Baixo, 9100 Santa Cruz 291 524933
Daily 9.00 a.m. - midnight

Tourist Office, Ribeira Brava, Forte de São Bento, 9350 **Ribeira Brava** 291 951675
Mon to Fri 9.00 a.m. - 12.30 p.m. & 2.00 p.m. - 5.00 p.m. Sat 9.30 a.m. - 12.00 noon

Tourist Office, Porto Moniz, 9270 **Porto Moniz** 291 852594
Mon - Fri 10.00 a.m. - 3.00 p.m. Sat 12.00 p.m. - 3.00 p.m.

Tourist Office, Santana, Sitio do Serrado, 9230 **Santana** 291 572 992
Mon to Fri 9.00 a.m. - 12.30 p.m. & 2.00 p.m. - 5.30 p.m. Sat 9.30 a.m. - 12.00 noon

Tourist Office, Porto Santo 291 985189
Avenida Henrique Vieira e Castro, **Porto Santo** 9400
Mon to Fri 9.00 a.m. - 5.30 p.m. Sat 10.00 a.m. - 12.30 p.m.

APPENDIX B

GARDENS, NATURE RESERVES, NATURAL HISTORY MUSEUMS, FESTIVALS & EVENTS

GARDENS

Monte Palace Tropical Garden (and Museum) www.montepalace.com
Caminho do Monte, **Monte** Open daily (not Christmas Day) 9.30 a.m. - 6 p.m.

Monte Municipal Park Monte Open daily - no admission charge

Jardim Botânico da Madeira www.sra.pt/jarbot

Quinta do Bom Sucesso, **Funchal** Open daily (not Christmas Day) 9.00 a.m. - 6 p.m.

Quinta das Cruzes (gardens and museum) www.sra.pt/jarbot/
Santa Clara, **Funchal** Open Monday to Friday 10.00 a.m. - 12.30 p.m & 2.00p.m - 5.30pm

Quinta Vigia, Avenida do Infante www.sra.pt/jarbot

Parque de Santa Catarina, **Funchal** Monday to Friday 9.00 a.m. - 5 p.m.

Municipal Dona Amélia Garden, Avenida Arriaga, **Funchal** www.sra.pt/jarbot

Municipal Garden Avenida Arriaga, **Funchal** Public park - no admission charge

Parque de Santa Catarina, Funchal Open daily - no admission charge

Palheiro Gardens www.madeira-gardens.com
Palheiro Ferreiro Open Monday to Friday 9.00 a.m. - 5.30 p.m.

Quinta da Boa Vista, Rua do Lombo da Boa Vista
Funchal Open Monday to Saturday 9.00 a.m. - 5.30 p.m.

Orchid Garden, Rua Pita da Silva, **Funchal** www.madeiraorchids.com
Open daily 9.30 a.m. - 6 p.m.
Quinta Magnólia Gardens Rua do Dr Pita, **Funchal** Open daily - no admission charge

Quinta da Serra close to the square, **Santo da Serra** Open daily - no admission charge

NATURE RESERVES

Parque Ecológico do Funchal   291 784700
(No admission charge)

Núcleo de Dragoeiros das Neves - São Gonçalo   291 795155
(No admission charge) Opening Hours: Daily 9.00 a.m. - 6.00 p.m.

Parque Florestal Ribeiro Frio   (No admission charge) Open daily

Espaço Natural Floresta Laurissilva   291 854033

Chão da Ribeira, Seixal, Porto Moniz   (No admission charge) Open daily

Rocha do Navio Nature Reserve - Santana

NATURAL HISTORY MUSEUMS

Museu Municipal do Funchal (Natural History Museum and Aquarium)   291 229761
In the beautiful Palácio de São Pedro. Permanent exhibitions of fauna, flora and geology including fish, bird and mammal specimens, insects, plants, minerals, rocks and fossils.
Opening hours: Daily (except Mondays) 10.00 a.m. - 6.00 p.m.

Aquário da Madeira Porto Moniz   www.aquariodamadeira.com
Opening Hours: Daily 9.00 a.m. - 6.00 p.m

Volcano Centre and Caves São Vicente Opening Hours: Daily 9.00 a.m. - 7.00 p.m.

Núcleo Museológico - Rota da Cal (The Lime Route) Open daily   291 842023

Museu da Baleia (Whale Museum)   91 961858
Situated in Caniçal in a new purpose-built building, the museum is a testament to the history of Madeiran whaling. Open daily (except Mondays) 10.00 am - 6.00 pm

THINGS TO DO Note: this list is not exhaustive

Sailing/whale & dolphin watching & trips to the Desertas Islands

Gavião-Viagens Turisticas Lda (Gavião Luxury Yacht)   291 241124 / 919916303
Marina do Funchal, 9000-055 Funchal   gaviaomadeira@netmadeira.com

Bonita da Madeira "Dream Cruises"   291 762 218 919183829
Estrada Monumental 187   info@bonita-da-madeira.com
9000-100 Funchal   www.bonita-da-madeira.com

Sailing/whale & dolphin watching

Beluga Submarine Vision - Glass Bottom Boat   967 044217

Visões Aquadélicas. Lda   belugasubmarine@hotmail.com

Ilhéu Ketch departs from Calheta/Madalena da Mar   291 974044/968 768194
Contact skipper: João Vieira   www.ilheu-sailing.com   joaovilheu@hotmail.com

Ribeira Brava - restored fishing vessel   963 103 762/291 771582

Lobosonda, Calheta Marine, Calheta   lobosonda@sapo.pt

Santa Maria (Replica of Columbus' vessel)   291 220327
Marina - Funchal, 9000-055 Funchal   nau.santa.maria@mail.telepac.pt
Sea Born Sea Born Kiosk   291 231312/919 916 221

Marina do Funchal   seaborn@madeira.com

Bird Watching

Horizonte do Atlántico, Rua do Quebra Costas, 28   291 280033/963 390796
9000-034 Funchal   www.venturadomar@iol.pt www.venturadomar.com

Madeira Wind Birds, Rua da Pena, 10 G   917777441
9050-099 Funchal   info@madeirabirds.com www.madeirabirds.com

Climbing & Canyoning

Horizonte do Atlántico, Rua do Quebra Costas, 28, 2   963 390796/291 280033
9000-034 Funchal   www.venturadomar.com www.venturadomar@iol.pt

Nuno Cunha Canyoning Guide   966256395/962837491
Calhua, São Jorge   cardosoecunha@gmail.com

FESTIVALS/ANNUAL EVENTS

For exact dates when each of these annual events will take place, see   www.visitmadeira.pt

Walking Festival	January
Carnival	mid-February
Flower Festival (3 day event)	end of April/early May
Atlantic Festival	June
Wine Festival	end August/beginning September
Festival of the Bands	mid-October
Christmas Lights/New Year Celebrations	December/January

APPENDIX C (1) OFFICIAL RECOMMENDED TRAILS FOR HIKERS

PR01	Vereda do Areeiro	PR10	Levada do Furado
PR01.1	Vereda da Ilha	PR11	Vereda dos Balcões
PR01.2	Vereda do Pico Ruivo -	PR12	Caminho Real da Encumeada
PR01.3	Vereda do Encumeada -	PR13	Vereda do Fanal
PR02	Vereda do Urzal	PR14	Levada dos Cedros
PR03	Vereda do Burro	PR15	Vereda da Ribeira da Janela
closed until further notice		PR16	Levada da Fajã do Rodriques
PR03.1	Vereda do Monte	PR17	Caminho do Pináculo e Folhadal
PR04	Vereda do Barreiro	PR18	Levada do Rei
closed until further notice		PR19	Caminho Real do Paúl do Mar
PR05	Vereda das Fundoras	PR20	Vereda do Jardim do Mar
PR06	Levada das 25 Fontes	PR21	Caminho do Norte
PR06.1	Levada do Risco	(Encumeada - Ribeira Grande)	
PR07	Levada do Moinho	PR22	Vereda do Chão dos Louros
PR08		(São Vicente valley)	
Vereda da Ponta de São Lourenço		PR23	Levada da Azenha
PR09	Levada do Caldeirão Verde	- Caminho Velho do Castelo - (Caniçal)	

APPENDIX C (2) DISABLED ROUTES

"Tourism and leisure activities have become basic aspects of modern society. The right to enjoy them is a quality of life indicator and an element of social integration, just as the right to education and work.
Leisure enjoyment forms part of a satisfying human experience and is fundamental for the physical, psychological and social development of the individual. In the case of the disabled, moreover, it can be considered a vitally important factor towards complete integration."
           (Taken from the Tourmac website, www.tourmac.info/discapacided/index)

The above sets out the philosophy behind this imaginative programme, funded by the

European Union and the Spanish and Portuguese Governments who have acquired the (*Joelette*) cycles so that the disabled can enjoy hiking in this part of the world. The *Joelettes* (adapted wheelchairs) are offered free of charge to both locals and visitors, so that no member of the family needs to miss out when the rest go walking. These routes are not suitable for normal wheelchair access; however, use of the adapted cycles requires either previous experience, or the services of the specialized guides.

The Madeiran programme is managed by the Forestry Service in conjunction with the Fire and Ambulance Service (The *Bombeiros*) and currently offers two established routes signed with PB JOELLETTE information panels, field code markings and fingerposts.

PBTTJOELETTE - From **Portela** to **Fajã dos Rolos** (close to Machico Distance 12.6 km Descent 165 m. Follows and intersects with Walk 50 in Walk! Madeira - Volume 2 (PR5 - Vereda das Funduras).

PR JOEL - **Queimadas** (Santana) to **Pico das Pedras** Distance 2.1 km - Descent/Ascent 20 m. For directions see Walk 20 in this publication.

ROUTE FOR THE BLIND: PR JOEL - **Queimadas** (Santana) to **Pico das Pedras** Distance 2.1 km - Descent/Ascent 20 m. For directions see Walk 20 in this publication.

Contacts: -
Direcção Regional de Turismo de Madeira, Avenida Arriaga 18 Funchal   291 211900

Direcção Regional das Florestas/Secretaria Regional Ambiente Recourses Naturais
Sra. Eng. Ana Sé   Tel: 291 740060 Fax: 291 740065

Associação dos Bombeiros Voluntários da Calheta Sr. João Alegria, Comandante
Corporação dos Bombeiros da Calheta   Tel: 291 827204 Fax: 291 827392 Mob: 96 4785443

Associação dos Bombeiros Voluntários da Santana Sr. Nuno - Adjunto do Comandante da Corporação dos Bombeiros Santana, Sr. José Antonio Freitas - Comandante
                                        Tel: 291 570110 Fax: 291570119 Mob: 964786895

Casado Povo de Machico Sr Emanuel Spinola - Presidente da Casa do Povo de Machico
                                        Tel: 291 966098 Fax: 291 966384 Mob: 913 458384

CYCLING ROUTES

PBTTJOELETTE - From **Portela** to **Fajã dos Rolos** (eastern route close to Machico) Distance 12.6 km - Descent 165 m. Follows and intersects with our Walk 50 (PR5 - Verada das Funduras)

PBTT1 - From **Cruzinhas**, **Fonte do Bispo** to **São Lourenço**, **Fajã da Ovelha** (western route starting close to the Forestry Post at Fonte do Bispo; off the ER210). Descent c.700m

PBTT2 - **Lombada dos Cedros** (northern route starting from Fonte do Bispo) - Details not available at time of printing.

APPENDIX D - REFERENCE SOURCES

MAPS

Madeira Tour & Trail Super-Durable Map (pub. Discovery Walking Guides Ltd.). Regularly re-researched and updated, highly detailed and accurate. For the latest version see www.dwgwalking.co.uk or www.amazon.co.uk

Madeira Bus & Touring Map (pub. Discovery Walking Guides Ltd.). For the latest edition see websites as above.

Shirley Whitehead's Madeira Walks (2nd Edition) (ISBN 978190494655 pub. 2011 Discovery Walking Guides Ltd).
Walk! Madeira (3rd edition) (ISBN 9781904946694 pub. 2010 Discovery Walking Guides Ltd.)

REFERENCE BOOKS
Flora Endémica da Madeira (Roberto Jardim/David Fransisco pub.2000 ISBN 9728622007)
Madeira Plants and Flowers (L O Franquinho/A Da Costa pub.1999 ISBN 972917721X)
Madeira's Natural History in a Nutshell (Peter Sziemer pub.2000 ISBN 9729177317)
Madeira - A Botanical Melting Pot (Dr Susanne Lipps pub.2006 ISBN 3938282096)
SPEA - Where to Watch Birds in the Madeira Archipelago (Cláudia Delgado pub.2006 ISBN 9729901899)
Prion Birdwatchers' Guide to Portugal and Madeira (H Costa, C C Moore, G Elias (pub. Prion Birdwatchers' Guide)
Field Guide to the Birds of the Atlantic Islands: Canary Islands, Madeira, Azores, Cape Verde (Tony Clarke, Chris Orgill (Illustrator), Tony Disley pub.2006 Christopher Helm Publishers Ltd ISBN 0713660236)
A Field Guide to the Butterflies of the Ecological Park and Madeiran Archipelago (Andrew Wakeham-Dawson, Michael Salmon, António Franquinho Aguiar - published by the Câmara Municipal do Funchal

BOOK SHOPS
Fundação Livraria Esperança -Rua dos Ferreiros 119 & 156 Funchal (close to Municipal Square) Tel: 291 221 116
Established in 1886, this is the oldest bookshop in Portugal with over 100,000 titles including a good selection of walking guides, maps and historical and environment publications.

PUBLICATIONS FOR BIRD WATCHING ENTHUSIASTS
SPEA-Madeira Discover the Birds of Laurissilva IBA (and surrounding areas)
Discover the Birds of Ponta do Pargo IBA
- available from SPEA-Madeira (Portuguese Society for the Protection of Birds, Travessa das Torres, Old Town, 9060-314 Funchal Tel: 291 241 210 www.spea.pt madeira@spea.pt
Discover the Birds of Funchal Ecological Park   Parque Ecológico do Funchal Madeira

DVDs
Footloose on Madeira DVD - Grindelwald Productions - Part of a 20 episode TV series 'Footloose in Europe"
Produced by David and Debra Rixon, this full length DVD includes a brief history of the island plus a comprehensive tour and a walking travelogue of Madeira's highlights.
Available from Amazon UK £9.99

APPENDIX E BUS INFORMATION

Madeira's network of bus services is cheap, usually punctual and is a fun way to see the island and to access some of the walking routes, but service provision varies significantly with the most frequent and accessible services being in and around **Funchal** and along the south coastal towns between **Ribeira Brava** in the west and **Machico** in the east. Other bus routes to the west, northwest and northeastern areas of the island are infrequent and extremely slow so it's important to check out the times before hand. There are no bus services to the central area across **Paúl da Serra**, **Rabaçal** and **Fanal**, nor in the central east to the mountainous areas of **Areeiro**, **Ruivo** and **Teixeira**.

Finding the appropriate bus can be confusing as several operators run the services. The current bus operators and route numbers are set out below, but as timetables frequently change it's important that you pick up the latest timetables at one of the information/ticket kiosks along the main **Avenida do Mar** or from the **Lido** area, or the Tourist Offices.

Bus Company	Livery	
CITY SIGHTSEEING BUS	Red	www.city-sightseeing.com
SIGHTSEEING BUS	Yellow	www.yellowbustours.com

HORÁRIOS	Orange	www.horariosdofunchal.pt
H/SÃO GONÇALO	Silver/White/Orange	www.horariosdofunchal.pt
SAM	Green/Cream	www.sam.pt
RODOESTE	Red/Cream	www.rodoeste.pt
EACL	Red/White/Grey	www.eacl.pt

Funchal Bus Stops

All buses depart and return along **Avenida do Mar/Avenida das Comunidades Madeirenses** and all services, except SAM, have bus stops in Old Town close to the *teleférico*. SAM buses also depart and return from the bus terminus on **Avenida Calouste Gulbenkian** across from D**olca Vita Shopping Centre**.

Island Bus Routes (including those compatible with the walking routes)

R +H	Câmara de Lobos	1 3 4 6 7 8 80 96 107 115 123 137 139 142 146 148 154
R	Estreito de Câmara de Lobos	3 4 6 7 8 80 96 107 115 123 137 139 142 146
R	Jardim do Serra/Corticeiros	3 96
R	Cabo Girão	4 6 7 80 96 107 115 139 142 146 154
R	Ribeira Brava	4 6 7 80 96 107 115 139 142 146
R	Ponta do Sol	4 80 107 115 142 146
R	Calheta	80 107 115 142
R	Prazeres	80 107 115 142
R	Jardim do Mar/Paúl do Mar	80 107 142
R	Ponto do Pargo	80 107 142
R	Achadas da Cruz	80 107
R	Porto Moniz/Santa	80 139 **150**
R	São Vicente	6 139
R+HSG	Arco de São Jorge	6 103 138
R	Encumeada	6 139
H	Curral das freiras/Eira do Serrado	81
H	Madeira Shopping	8 16 50
H	Monte	20 21 48
H	Babosas	22
HSG	Ecological Park	56 103 138
HSG	Ribeiro Frio	56 103 138
H	Curral Romeiros	29
H	Botanical Gardens	29 30 31
H	Palheiro Gardens	36A 37
HSG	Camacha	129
HSG	São Jorge/Santana	56 103 138
S	Caniço/Santa Cruz	20 **25** 53 113 156
S	Machico	20 23 53 78 113 156
S	Maroços	156 **203**
S	Caniçal/São Lourenço Peninsula	113
S+HSG	Santa da Serra	20 25 77 **78**
S	Portela	53 78
S+HSG	Faial	53 56 78 103 138
S+HSG	Porto Cruz	53 56 78 103 138 **207** 208
AC	Caniço	**2 136 155**

R = Rodoeste
H = Horários
HSG = Horários/Carros de São Gonçalo - an affiliated company of Horários
S = SAM
AC = Automóveis Caniçal

Note:
Bus numbers in bold print refer to local services only - all other routes are to and from Funchal

PLACE NAMES INDEX

The following index includes place names in Portuguese and some of the most commonly used English equivalents.

25 Fontes	6, 95, 96, 123, 124, 149	Avenida do Mar	146, 151, 152
		Avenida dos Pescadores	144
A			
Abrigo do Pastor	81, 83	**B**	
Abrigo do Poiso Restaurant	87	Babosas	4, 14, 17, 44, 47, 48, 52, 53, 146, 152
Achada de Santo Antão	100		
Achada do Teixeira	78	Balcões	4, 76, 77, 90, 149
Achadas da Cruz	6, 126, 128, 152		
		Banda de Além	72
Ameixieiras	84-86	Bar Achada	119
Amparo	39, 135, 146	Bar Encumeada	31, 32, 33
Antigo Fio da Fajã da Ovelha	143, 144	Bar Flor da Selva	77
		Bar Flõr Rochão	77
Aquário da Madeira	15, 129, 148	Bar Maktub	144
Arco da Calheta	100, 101	Bar Poleiro	144
Arco de São Jorge	4, 14, 59, 60, 78, 152	Bar Santa Rita	38
		Bar/Rest São Cristovão	61
Areeiro (Pico)	5, 9, 44, 87-89, 120, 149, 151	Bica da Cana	5, 6, 105-107, 111, 120, 122
		Boa Morte	140, 141
Assomada	54	Boaventura	4, 59, 60

Boca da Encumeada	31, 105, 107	Senhora da Conceição	26, 71, 131
Bom Sucesso	4, 48-50, 53, 147	Capela de Nossa Senhora de Fátima	97, 101
Botanical Gardens	17, 28, 48, 49, 53, 152	Capela de Nossa Senhora de Saúde	86
Botánico Teleférico	52, 53	Capela Nossa Senhora da Saudé	86

C

Cabeço Furado	90, 92	Capela Nossa Senhora de Piedade	57
Cabo	6, 132, 135, 139-141	Capela Nossa Senhora do Boa Morte	140, 141
Cabo Girão	3, 9, 15, 17, 18, 34, 36, 39, 146, 152	Capela Nossa Senhora do Monte	44
		Captain's Bar	56
Cabo Girão Sky Walk	18, 36	Casa Branca	39
Caldeirão Verde	78-80, 149	Casa das Queimadas	80
Calheta	6, 16, 97, 100, 101, 123, 125, 126, 142, 146, 148, 150, 152	Casa de Abrigo das Queimadas	78, 80
		Casa de Chá	132, 135, 141
Calheta Hydro Power	97	Caves of São Vicente (grutas)	15
Calvario	44	Chão da Ribeira da Seixal	104, 148
Camacha	28, 81, 85, 146, 152	Chão dos Louros Park	108, 109
Cãmara de Lobos	17, 18, 24-27, 34, 36, 146, 151	Choupana Hills Hotel	28, 29
		Churchill Place Restaurant	26
Caminho da Pereira	85	Ciência Viva Centre	129
Caminho da Quinta	72	Colina da Fajã Hotel	133, 142
Caminho das Babosas	47, 52	Coral Restaurant	26
Caminho do Monte	47, 147	Corrego do Ilhéu	74
Caminho do Norte (PR21)	108, 109, 149	Cova Grande Valley	66
Caminho do Pico	129-131, 138	Cristo Rei	5, 17, 100, 102, 105, 107
Caminho do Pináculo e Folhadal (PR17)	32, 149	Cruz	68
Caminho do Velha	139, 140	Cruz da Caldeira	34, 36
Caminho Madre de Agua	86	Curral	41, 42
Caminho Real da Encumeada (PR12)	149	Curral das Freiras (Nun's Valley)	4, 41, 42, 89, 152
Caminho Real do Monte	4, 44, 149		
Caminho Real do Paúl do Mar (PR19)	149	Curral dos Romeiros	49, 152
		Curral Falso	6, 114, 116, 117, 119
Caminho Velho do Castelo	4, 54, 149	Curral Romeiros	4, 51, 152
Canhas	146	Curral Valley	41, 42
Caniçal	4, 55-57, 65-67, 71-75, 146, 148, 149, 152, 153	**D**	
		Deserta Grande	15
		Desertas Islands	9, 11, 15, 21, 24, 35, 65, 71, 148
Caniço	54, 146, 152		
Capela Coração de Jesus	84, 86		
Capela de Nossa			

Dolca Vita Shopping Centre	152
Dona Amélia Garden Jardim (Gardens)	16, 147

E

Eagle Rock (Penha d"Aguia)	18, 68-70, 77, 88, 92
Ecological Park	4, 8, 44, 52, 86, 87, 151, 152
Ecological Park Reception Centre	89
Eira do Serrado	4, 41-43, 89, 152
Encumeada	3, 31, 100, 105, 108, 109, 111, 114, 120, 122, 149, 152
Encumeada Pass	31, 100, 105, 106, 108
Encumeada Snack Bar	31-33
Encumeada Water House	33
Espaço Natural Floresta Laurissilva	148
Estalagem	41, 42
Estanquinhos	5, 111-113
Estanquinhos Forestry House	112
Estrada da Banda d'Além	67
Estrada Monumental	24, 25, 39, 146-148
Estreito de Camâra de Lobos	3, 34, 36, 146, 152
Estrela da Calheta	123, 146

F

Faial	18, 68, 70, 77, 78, 88, 91, 93, 146, 152
Fajã da Noguiera	77, 88
Fajã da Ovelha	6, 132, 133, 142-144
Fajã da Rocha do Navio	62
Fajã dos Padros	17
Fajã dos Rolos	150
Fanal	5, 6, 103, 104, 114, 117, 151
Fanal Forestry Post	114
Fanal Posto Florestal	114
Fátima (chapel)	5, 100, 101
Figueirinha	82
Fish Hatchery	77
Floresta Laurissilva	148
Folhadal	32, 149
Fonte do Bispo	115, 150
Fontes Ruivos	112, 113
Fortaleza do São Trigo (fort)	16
Fortim do Faial	18
Forum Shopping Centre	39, 146
Funchal	3, 4, 11, 13-18, 24, 27-31, 34, 36-39, 41, 42, 44, 46-48, 50-52, 54, 56, 60, 62, 65, 71, 78, 85-87, 89, 90, 93, 108, 129, 132, 136, 139, 142, 146-153
Funchal Ecological Park	8, 86, 87, 89, 151

G

Garachico	35, 36
Garajau	17
Golden Gate Café	16
Grutas de São Vicente (caves)	15

H

Horténsia Tea Rooms	29
Hotel Monumental Lido	27
Hotel Orca Praia	25

I

Ice House (Poço da Neve)	89
Igreja	144
Igreja de Nossa Senhora do Monte (church)	44
Ilha	78
Ilhas Desertas	9, 11, 15, 21, 24, 35, 65, 71, 148
Ilhéu da Rocha do Navio	62
Ilhéu Mole	130
Ilhéu Preto	60
Ilhéu Vermelho	60

Ilhéus da Ribeira da Janela	117	Levada do Alecrim	97, 98
		Levada do Bom Sucesso	48-50
J		Levada do Caldeirão Verde	78-80, 149
Janela	6, 95-98, 103, 117, 119, 136, 146	Levada do Caniçal	4, 65
		Levada do Castelejo	4, 68
		Levada do Curral	37
Janela Valley	95-98, 104, 115, 118	Levada do Facho	36
		Levada do Furado (PR10)	5, 90, 93, 149
Jardim Botánico (Botanic Gardens)	17, 28, 48, 49, 52, 53, 151, 152	Levada do Moinho (PR7)	6, 126, 149
		Levada do Norte	3, 31, 32, 34, 36
Jardim Botánico da Madeira	147	Levada do Paúl	5, 100, 105
		Levada do Portela	92
Jardim da Serra	34, 35	Levada do Rei (PR18)	149
Jardim do Mar	7, 149	Levada do Risco (PR6.1)	5, 95, 124, 149
Jasmin Tea House	3, 28, 30		
João Gomes	49, 50, 52, 53	Levada dos Cedros (PR14)	6, 103, 114, 117, 149
Juncal	5, 87, 88		
Junqueira	126	Levada dos Piornais	3, 37, 40
		Levada dos Tornos	4, 28, 48, 51-53, 84, 86
L			
Ladeira da Casa Branca	39		
Lagoa da Portela	92	Levada Nova	38, 132, 142
Lagoa do Vento	95, 98	Levada Velha	76
Lajeado	99, 1	Lido	3, 24, 37, 146, 147, 151
Lamaceiros	6, 15, 93, 126, 136, 138, 146		
		Lombada dos Cedros	150
Lamaceiros forestry house	92, 93	Lombada Velha	140, 141
		Lombo Chão	42
Lamaceiros water house	92, 136	Lombo da Quinta	3
Largo da República	26	Lombo do Salão	123
Largo do Fonte	44, 47	Lombo dos Faias	92
Largo do Poço	27	Lombo dos Marinheiros	133
Largos dos Miradouros	146	Lombo Grande	70
Levada da Bica da Cana	105, 106	Lombo Quinedo	139, 140
Levada da Fajã do Rodrigues (PR16)	149	**M**	
Levada da Ribeira da Janela	6, 118, 126, 136	Macapez	142, 143
		Machico	4, 17, 56, 65, 71-73, 74, 90, 146, 150-152
Levada da Rocha Vermelha	96, 124, 125		
		Madalena do Mar	148
Levada da Serra	77, 120, 121	Madeira Shopping	3, 37, 40, 152
Levada da Serra do Faial	93	Madeira Theme Park	78
Levada das 25 Fontes (PR6)	6, 95, 96, 123, 149	Madre de Agua	5, 84, 86
		Maroços	146, 152
Levada das Cales	46	Metada Valley	77
Levada das Rabaças	3, 31-33	Miradouro da Portela Bar/Restaurant	92
Levada de Baixo	69, 70	Moinho	6, 126, 149

Monte	4, 13, 17, 28, 44, 47, 48, 51, 52, 87, 89, 146, 147, 149, 152	Parque das Queimadas Parque de Santa Catarina Parque Ecológico do Funchal	147, 152 79 147 4, 8, 44, 52, 86, 87, 148, 151, 152
Monte Palace Tropical Gardens	13, 47, 51, 52, 147		
Monumental Lido	27, 39, 147	Parque Natural da Madeira	9, 62
Museu da Baleira	75, 148		
Museu Municipal do Funchal	148	Paúl da Serra	10, 31, 95, 100, 103, 105, 111, 113, 114, 117, 120, 123,126, 129, 136, 151
Museums	6, 14, 15, 75, 129, 147, 148		
N			
Ninho da Manta	87-89	Paúl do Mar	6, 132, 142-144, 146, 149, 152
Nogueira	36, 77, 88		
Nossa Senhora de Boa Morte (chapel)	140, 141	Pedregal	139, 141
Nossa Senhora de Conceição	26, 27, 71, 131	Penha d'Aguia (Eagle Rock)	18, 68-70, 77, 88, 92
Nossa Senhora de Fátima (chapel)	5, 97, 101	Pico Alto Pico da Piedade	45, 46 4, 56
Nossa Senhora de Piedade	57	Pico das Favas Pico das Pedras	134, 135, 139 5, 78, 79, 150
Nossa Senhora do Monte	44	Pico das Torres Pico do Areeiro	9, 68 5, 87, 89, 120
Nosso Senhor da Montanha	102	Pico do Cedro Pico do Facho	70 4, 71-74
Núcleo de Dragoeiros das Neves	14, 148	Pico do Suna Pico dos Barcelos	92 42
Núcleo Museológico	148	Pico Grande	31, 32, 43
Nun's Valley (Curral das Freiras)	4, 41, 42, 89, 152	Pico Rabaçal Pico Ruivo	99 5, 9, 22, 68, 77, 78, 111, 112, 120, 149
O		Pico Ruivo do Paúl	5, 111, 112
O Farol	132, 135, 141	Pináculo	6, 32, 120-122, 149
Orca Praia Hotel	25		
Orchid Garden	147	Pinheiro das Voltas	37
Our Lady of Monte Church	48	Poço da Neve (Ice House)	89
Our Lady of Peace	46	Poiso	5, 44, 81, 87
P		Ponta do Pargo	6, 132, 135, 139, 141, 142, 146, 151
Palácio de São Pedro	148		
Palácio e Fortaleza de São Lourenço	16	Ponta do Sol	107, 117, 132, 146, 152
Palheiro Ferreiro	147	Portas da Vila	126, 129
Palheiro Gardens	14, 28, 30,		

Madeira Walks 1 157

Portela	5, 77, 90, 92, 93, 146, 150, 152
Portela A Vista Bar	92
Porto Cruz	70, 92, 146, 152
Porto da Cruz	17, 18, 68, 92
Porto Moniz	6, 15, 17, 60, 117, 126, 129-131, 136, 138, 146-148, 152
Porto Santo	9, 12, 147
Posto Florestal da Santa	126
Posto Florestal Nature Reserve	77
PR 1 Vereda do Areeiro	87, 88, 89, 149
PR 1.1 Vereda da Ilha	149
PR 1.2 Vereda do Pico Ruivo	149
PR 1.3 Vereda do Encumeada	149
PR 3 Vereda do Burro	149
PR 3.1 Caminho Real do Monte	4, 44, 149
PR 4 Vereda do Barreiro	149
PR 5 Vereda das Funduras	149
PR 6 Levada das 25 Fontes	6, 95, 96, 123, 149
PR 6.1 Levada do Risco	5, 95, 124, 149
PR 7 Levada do Moinho	6, 126, 149
PR 8 Vereda da Ponta de São Lourenço	149
PR 9 Levada do Caldeirão Verde	78-80, 149
PR10 Levada do Furado	5, 90, 93, 149
PR11 Vereda dos Balcões	4, 76, 90, 149
PR12 Caminho Real da Encumeada	149
PR13 Vereda do Fanal	103, 149
PR14 Levada dos Cedros	6, 103, 114, 117, 149
PR15 Vereda da Ribeira da Janela	103, 149
PR16 Levada da Fajã do Rodrigues	149
PR17 Caminho do Pináculo e Folhadal	32, 149
PR18 Levada do Rei	149
PR19 Caminho Real do Paúl do Mar	149
PR20 Vereda do Jardim do Mar	149
PR21 Caminho do Norte	108, 109, 149
PR22 Vereda do Chão dos Louros	108, 149
Praia Formosa	3, 24, 25
Praia Restaurant	25
Prainha	4, 56
Prazeres	132, 146, 152

Q

Queimadas	5, 78, 150
Quinta da Boa Vista	147
Quinta da Serra	84, 148
Quinta das Cruzes	147
Quinta das Eiras	85
Quinta do Arco Rose Garden	14
Quinta do Bom Sucesso	147
Quinta do Ferreiro	28
Quinta do Lorde	56-58
Quinta do Terreiro da Luta Restaurant	47
Quinta Gorick	29
Quinta Serrado das Ameixieiras	85
Quinta Vigia	147
Quinta Vigia	16, 147

R

Rabaçal	5, 95, 97, 100, 101, 105, 123, 124, 136, 151
Rabaçal Forestry House	95, 124
Rabaçal Nature Spot Café	95
Rabaçal Posto Florestal	95, 124
Rancho	17, 78-80
Reid's Hotel	16, 89
Reid's Palace Hotel	16, 89
Reservatória Achadas da Cruz	128
Residential Encumeada Hotel	32
Resort Quinta do Lorde	56-58
Restaurant Churchill Place	26

Restaurant Coral	26	Rua Mary Jane Wilson	86
Restaurante Abrigo do Pastor	81	Rua Nossa Senhora da Conceição	27
Restaurante O Arco	59, 60	Rua Padre João Pedro Gomes Henriques	85
Ribeira Bezerro	91	Rua São João de Deus	26
Ribeira Brava	14, 18, 31, 32, 34, 36, 59, 108, 109, 120, 126, 129, 132, 136, 139, 142, 146-148, 151, 152	Ruivo	5, 9, 22, 68, 77, 78, 87-89, 111-113, 120, 149, 151
		Ruivo do Paúl	5, 111, 112
Ribeira da Cruz	126, 128	**S**	
Ribeira da Janela	6, 95-97, 99, 103, 114, 115, 117-119, 126, 136, 146, 149	Santa	37, 115, 126, 129-131, 136, 138, 152
Ribeira da Vaca	139	Santa Catarina	16, 147
		Santa Catarina Park	16
Ribeira das Cales	44, 52, 89	Santa Clara	147
Ribeira das Galinhas	144	Santa Cruz	17, 54, 146, 147, 152
Ribeira de João Gomes	49, 50, 52, 53		
Ribeira de São Roque	68	Santa Forestry Post	126
Ribeira do Alecrim	95	Santa Posto Florestal	126
Ribeira do Tristão	128	Santa Rita	3, 38, 40
Ribeira dos Marinheiros	133	Santana	4, 5, 17, 59, 60, 62, 64, 77-79, 90, 146-148, 150, 152
Ribeira Grande	5, 95, 97-99, 108, 109, 124, 149		
Ribeira Lajeado	99		
Ribeira Natal	75	Santo António da Serra	84
Ribeira Porco	59, 61	Santo da Serra	5, 84-86, 92-94, 146, 148
Ribeira Seca	146		
Ribeiro Frio	5, 14, 68, 76, 77, 90, 92, 93, 148, 152	São Cristovão	60, 61
		São Gonçalo	14, 148, 152, 153
Risco	5, 95, 96, 123, 124, 149	São João Fort	15, 129
		São Jorge	4, 14, 59, 60, 78, 149, 152
Risco Waterfall	96		
Rocha do Navio	62, 148	São Lourenço (peninsula)	4, 16, 56, 65, 66, 71, 74, 133, 149, 150, 152
Rocha do Navio Nature Reserve	62, 148		
Romeiros	3, 4, 28, 49, 51-53, 152		
		São Martinho	39, 42
Roque de Faial	69	São Roque	4, 68-70, 88, 91
Rota da Cal	15, 148		
Rua Antonio Costa Medico	50	São Roque do Faial	78, 88
Rua Arreiro	38	São Sebastião (church)	26
Rua da Banda de Além	72	São Trigo Fortress (Fortaleza)	16
Rua da Calão	75		
Rua da Igreja	62		
Rua das Eirinhas	133		

São Vicente	5, 15, 31, 59, 60, 108, 109, 113, 121, 136, 146, 148, 149, 152	Terreiro da Luta	44, 46, 47, 52
		Tourist Offices	147
		Travessa das Torres	151
		Travessa de Ribeira João Gomes	50
Sé Catedral	16, 150	Travessa de Santa Rita	40
Seixal	104, 148	Travessa do Pinheira das Voltas	37
Selvagens Islands	21		
Senhora do Monte (church)	44, 47, 52	Travessa do Tanque	37
		Travessa do Valente	39
Serra da Água	33	Túnel do Caniçal	65, 67, 71, 73
Serrado	4, 5, 41, 42, 84-86, 89, 139, 141, 147, 152	Túnel Encumeada	31
		V	
		Vereda da Ilha (PR1.1)	149
Serrado das Ameixieiras	5, 84-86	Vereda da Ponta de São Lourenço (PR8)	149
Sitio da Pereira	84, 86		
Sitio de São João	133, 142	Vereda da Ribeira da Janela (PR15)	103, 117, 149
Snack Bar A Latada	131		
Snack Bar Azenha	55	Vereda das Funduras (PR5)	149
Snack Bar Encumeada	31		
Snack Bar Pinheira das Voltas	40	Vereda do Areeiro (PR1)	87, 88, 89, 149
Snack Bar Santa Rita	38	Vereda do Barreiro (PR4)	149
Socorridos Valley	37		
Spring of the Shepherdess	47	Vereda do Burro (PR3)	149
		Vereda do Chão dos Louros (PR22)	108, 149
Sugar Loaf	120-122		
		Vereda do Encumeada (PR1.3)	149
T			
Taxi information	13, 146	Vereda do Fanal (PR13)	103, 149
Teixeira	78, 151	Vereda do Jardim do Mar	149
Teleférico, Achada da Cruz	17		
		Vereda do Pico Ruivo (PR1.2)	149
Teleférico, Babaosas to Jardim Botanico	14, 17, 44, 48, 51, 52, 53		
		Vereda dos Balcões (PR11)	4, 76, 90, 149
Teleférico, Garajau to beach	17	Vermelho	140, 141
		Via Rápida	37, 38, 48-50
Teleférico, Rancho	17	Volcano Centre	15, 148
Teleférico, Rocha do Navio, Santana	17, 62, 63	**W**	
		Whale Museum	75, 148
Teleférico, sea front to Monte	17		